INFERNO
DECODED

Michael Haag

WITH
GREG WARD

Gallery Books

New York   London   Toronto   Sydney   New Delhi

Gallery Books
A Division of Simon & Schuster, Inc.
1230 Avenue of the Americas
New York, NY 10020

Chapter 8 © Paul McMahon 2013
Chapters 7, 9 and 13 © Greg Ward 2013
All other text copyright © Michael Haag 2013

Originally published in 2013 in Great Britain by Profile Books Ltd.

First Gallery Books trade paperback edition August 2013

GALLERY BOOKS and colophon are registered trademarks of
Simon & Schuster, Inc.

For information about special discounts for bulk purchases,
please contact Simon & Schuster Special Sales at 1-866-506-1949
or business@simonandschuster.com.

The Simon & Schuster Speakers Bureau can bring authors to your
live event. For more information or to book an event contact the
Simon & Schuster Speakers Bureau at 1-866-248-3049 or visit our
website at www.simonspeakers.com.

Manufactured in the United States of America

10 9 8 7 6 5 4 3 2 1

Library of Congress Cataloging-in-Publication Data is available.

ISBN 978-1-4767-5344-7
ISBN 978-1-4767-5186-3 (ebook)

To Beata Dasha

ACKNOWLEDGEMENTS

This book has followed Dan Brown's *Inferno* in using the William Wadsworth Longfellow translation of the *Divine Comedy*, though sometimes I have adapted it for clarity. Where occasionally Dan Brown has used Allen Mandelbaum's modern verse translation of the *Divine Comedy*, published by Bantam (originally University of California Press, 1980), that has been followed here too. Also I have occasionally used the prose translation of the *Divine Comedy* by John D Sinclair published by Oxford University Press (1939). Quotations from Dante's *Vita Nuova* are from the translation by Dante Gabriel Rossetti (1874).

For his help and advice I give my thanks to Alexei Grishin.

Thanks to Greg Ward (www.gregward.info) who wrote chapters Seven, Nine and Thirteen of this book. Paul McMahon kindly gave permission to adapt and shorten the chapter on 'Was Malthus Right?' from his book *Feeding Frenzy* (Profile Books, 2013) for use as Chapter Eight of this book.

Photographs: p.224 and p.233, Corbis Images; p.167 Karl Gruber; p.177 Russ London. All photographs of Florence and the Hagia Sophia were taken by Michael Haag.

The map of Florence on p.203 is taken from the *Blue Guide to Florence*, and has been adapted and reproduced with permission.

CONTƎNTS

Inferno Decoded

I n the heart of Florence a mysterious figure called the Shade throws himself from the bell tower of a church. But not before announcing his 'gift to mankind', a modern-day version of the Black Death, which will cull the world's human population by a third. The Shade calls his invention Inferno. 'The path to paradise passes directly through hell', he says. 'Dante taught us that.'

Dan Brown's *Inferno* is a tumultuous thriller, full of rapid twists and turns as Robert Langdon races through the streets and churches and secret passageways of Florence, unravelling the hidden meanings of verses and symbols in Dante's *Inferno* – and all the time following the *Map of Hell*, drawn by another great Florentine, Sandro Botticelli.

Inferno Decoded is an illuminating companion to Dan Brown's *Inferno*. It looks into the novel's darkest mysteries, sorting out the facts from the fiction and exploring the ancient cities that serve as its setting. Do the clues unveiled in symbology professor Robert Langdon's daring quest from Florence to Venice and Istanbul overlap with history? What codes and symbols did Dante employ in the *Divine Comedy* and which secret religious, philosophical, and scientific themes are hidden within his work? What lies behind Botticelli's *Mappa del'Inferno*?

Inferno Decoded also debates the big questions posed by Dan Brown. In a world that will soon be home to ten billion people, are we truly facing mass starvation, perpetual war and the collapse of human society? Does the Shade's plan to 'thin the human herd' make some sort of twisted sense? Does the future lie with the Transhumanist aim of genetically transforming ourselves into posthumans? And what lessons can be learned from the great humanists of the Renaissance themselves?

𝔇an 𝔅rown's 𝔍nferno

The darkest places in hell are reserved for those who maintain their neutrality in times of moral crisis.

Epigraph to Dan Brown's *Inferno*

At the heart of Dan Brown's *Inferno* lies a moral argument. According to one of the book's central characters, the world is overpopulated. Nothing effective has been done, or can be done using conventional means, to prevent the population increasing until Earth can no longer sustain such numbers and human society collapses under the strain.

This character, however, has a plan: a massive cull of the human population. After all, he remarks, the Black Death of 1348 amounted to much the same thing, and had wonderful results; the immediate increase in available land, and the redistribution of wealth into fewer hands, provided the stimulus that gave rise to the Renaissance. Faced with the choice between the collapse of civilised society on the one hand, and its rebirth on the other, would it really be such a bad thing if a modern version of the Black Death were set loose today?

This same character, first introduced as 'the Shade', sees images of that hellish world of overpopulation in Dante Alighieri's *Inferno*. In Dante's vision, the sufferings and anguish of the condemned are intensified by their sheer numbers: 'I ne'er would have believed / That ever Death so many had undone'. According to the Shade: 'To do nothing is to welcome Dante's hell ... cramped and starving, weltering in Sin.' Reminders of the plague leap out at Brown's perennial hero, Robert Langdon, in almost every street as he makes his way through Florence, seeking clues about the hidden doomsday device. 'My God,' Langdon thought, as he noticed a sign reading *La peste nera* (the Black Death), 'it's everywhere I turn!'

That sign was on Ghiberti's famous bronze doors, on the east side of the Baptistery, which had been commissioned as an offering to God in 1401 in the hope that Florence would be spared future epidemics. When Michelangelo saw the completed doors, he called them the Gates of Paradise. According to the Shade, however, 'The path to paradise passes directly through hell. Dante taught us that.'

In this introductory overview, we'll run through the essential plot, characters, themes and ideas of Dan Brown's *Inferno*. All are explored at greater length in the chapters that follow.

INTRODUCING THE SHADE

Florence lies in darkness, the Apennine mountains to the east shutting out the early rays of dawn. A desperate ghost-like figure runs along the banks of the River Arno and 'through the dolent city', 'through the eternal woe', his pursuers gaining ground, their footsteps growing louder.

This is how the Prologue of Dan Brown's *Inferno* begins – in the middle of things. Not only does Brown swiftly take us into his own plot, but he also draws us into the *Inferno* of Dante.

'Through the dolent city I flee...': the spire of the Badia, from which the Shade threw himself into the abyss.

'I am the Shade', cries the fleeing figure. For years he has been hunted, forced to live underground. Desperate to escape, he pauses briefly in the shadows of the Uffizi, then races north along the Via dei Castellani, around the back of the Palazzo Vecchio.

Opposite the looming bulk of the Bargello in the Via del Proconsolo, he throws himself against the iron gate at the base of the stairs of the ancient spire that rises above the church and cloisters of the Badia.

Into the narrow passage and up the spiralling marble staircase, the voices of his pursuers close behind him, the Shade clambers skywards, tormented by visions – lustful bodies writhing in fiery rain, the souls of gluttons floating in their own excrement, and far below the city, far below even the fires of Hell, in the frozen depths where Satan holds them in his icy grasp and devours them, are the traitors, the coldest and cruellest sinners of all. But there are darker places still, reserved for those who maintain their neutrality in times of moral crisis. The Shade knows there can be no return.

For Dante too there is no easy way. He must follow the Roman poet Virgil through Hell, where above its gates are inscribed these words, with their famous concluding line:

> *Through me the way is to the city dolent;*
> *Through me the way is to eternal woe;*
> *Through me the way among the people lost.*
> *Abandon all hope ye who enter here.*

In the course of the *Divine Comedy*, Dante descends through the ever-deeper circles of Hell. There he meets the shades of the damned – and there he reflects bitterly upon Florence, his native city, which has cast him into exile and sentenced him to death by burning at the stake if ever he returns. Only after passing through Hell and Purgatory is he cleansed of this world, and free to journey with his beloved Beatrice to the stars.

'Tell us where you've hidden it', the pursuing voices threaten. But the Shade is standing now on a narrow ledge high above the terracotta rooftops of Florence. They glow beneath him like a sea of fire, illuminating the fair landscape where giants like Giotto, Donatello, Brunelleschi, Michelangelo and Botticelli once roamed. He cries out, 'Guide me, dear Virgil, across the void.'

Suddenly, in these final moments, the Shade is startled by a face in the cobblestoned piazza hundreds of feet below. He sees her mournful eyes, in which he also senses a veneration for what he has accomplished, an understanding that he has no choice.

For the love of mankind he must protect his masterpiece, which even now waits, growing, simmering, beneath the blood-red waters of the infernal lagoon that reflects no stars.

Praying that the world will remember him not as a monstrous sinner but as a glorious saviour, and will appreciate the gift he has left behind, the Shade utters a final incantation: 'My gift is the future. My gift is salvation. My gift is Inferno.'

And whispering amen, he steps into the abyss.

The 'dolent city', the 'city of eternal woe', the city's rooftops glowing like a sea of fire; Dan Brown is reaching into Dante's *Inferno* for his own descriptions of Florence. The Badia, to which the Shade has fled, stood here in Dante's time, within a stone's throw of where he was born, its bells tolling the beginning and the end of each waking day. Each of those horrific visions that beset the Shade as he clambers up the spire is drawn from a circle of Dante's *Inferno*. 'Guide me Virgil', cries the Shade, just as Virgil guided Dante through the terrors of Hell. And Beatrice is there too; that mournful face far below, she is the Shade's beloved, his muse. But who is she really in the pages of Dan Brown's thriller. And what, precisely, is Inferno, the Shade's 'gift' to mankind?

THE PLOT UNFOLDS

Inferno is full of the exciting twists and turns you'd expect from Dan Brown, but in this case the plot is especially and devilishly deceptive.

The Prologue establishes the threat – the Shade has planted a device that will have earth-shattering consequences. But who is the Shade, what is the device, what is it meant to do – and where is it to be found, so that it can be neutralised in time?

No such thoughts are on Robert Langdon's mind, however, as he lies in a hospital bed, his head stitched up, his hair caked with blood. In fact he has nothing on his mind at all. First of all, he is unconscious. Then, when he awakes, he is suffering from amnesia – the consequence, he is told by the lissom Dr Sienna Brooks, of concussion after a bullet grazed his head.

Langdon too has visions, of a scalding red river, of Dante's 'river of boiling blood in which are steeped all who struck down their fellow men'. In Dante's *Inferno*, the poet crossed its churning waters into a terrifying landscape filled with thousands of writhing bodies suffering agonising deaths, roasted in fires, suffocating in faeces, being eaten alive – a landscape where, in Langdon's dream, a mysterious veiled woman reaches out her hands beseeching him for help, saying 'Seek and find'.

Langdon at this point knows nothing of the Shade or his infernal device. All he knows is that someone is trying to kill him. That's why he is in hospital, and that's why he spends three-quarters of the book on the run from his pursuers, gratifyingly accompanied by the willowy Sienna Brooks.

A Mesopotamian cylinder seal, much like the one Robert Langdon finds sewn into his jacket.

But why are they trying to kill him? It must have something to do with an ancient cylinder seal he has found sewn inside his jacket. Inside the seal, he discovers a minuscule self-powering projector that displays on the nearest wall Botticelli's *Mappa dell'Inferno*, illustrating Dante's *Inferno* and filled with tiny figures inhabiting the various circles of punishment, agony and pain. Professor of art history and symbology that he is, however, Robert Langdon cannot help noticing that Botticelli's original has been doctored. The sequence of the circles has been altered, and this must be a clue.

And so, the way you do when you're a famous symbologist, Langdon finds himself racing through the streets and secret passageways of Florence; a man on the run, pursued by black-uniformed soldiers with icy eyes and umlauts over their names, and by a spike-haired female motorbike rider clad in black leather, surveyed all the while by overhead drones. A man, too, who's given clues, one after the other – to what, he doesn't know, but if only he can find the answers then possibly they will explain his amnesia and why people are trying to kill him.

In due course, and almost without intention, Langdon picks up the scent among the clues left by the man who was the Shade, who turns out to have been the billionaire Swiss geneticist Bertrand Zobrist, a Dante enthusiast and the owner of Dante's death mask. Only then does Langdon realise that some great danger lies in Zobrist's infernal device, and that he has less than twenty-four hours to save the world. Which gives him something more to do, apart from avoiding getting shot and trying to remember why he came to Florence in the first place.

Inferno is a clever thriller, which operates on several planes at once, and is complicated still further when Langdon discovers that he is the victim of an elaborate theatrical event. Almost everyone he has encountered turns out to be someone else, actors on a stage, playing their parts in events that never happened, enacted for the sole purpose of trying to get Langdon to figure out where Zobrist has hidden his Inferno – which turns out to be a modern-day version of the Black Death. Zobrist believes that the world is overpopulated, and that within a few years it will become unsustainably so, leading to the total collapse of human society. Having observed that the Black Death pandemic of 1348 killed off a third of Europe's population, Zobrist has decided that the same exact proportion needs to be culled today.

The World Health Organisation wants to know where Zobrist has hidden his device so that they can deactivate it. In addition, however, a shadowy organisation called the Consortium, inconspicuously based on a colossal Mediterranean yacht, wants to know the same thing. Zobrist had hired the Consortium a year before he threw himself off the Badia tower, and tasked it with protecting his secrets, despite not knowing what those secrets may have been. When it learns that the WHO is using Langdon to find the location of Zobrist's Inferno, the Consortium wants to obtain that information too, to ensure that the device activates as Zobrist planned. And so its operatives kidnap Langdon, give him an injection or two, enmesh him in their play, and manipulate him through the greater part of the book as he tears along from Florence to Venice and Istanbul.

DANTE, BEATRICE AND FLORENCE

Three-quarters of Dan Brown's *Inferno* is set in Florence, and almost all of that takes place in what is described as 'the old city'. This was the city that lay within the thirteenth-century walls, the city that was Dante's world. Here he was born, and here in the great Baptistery he was baptised beneath the magnificent mosaic ceiling of heaven and hell. In Dante's day, the Duomo was newly under construction, while the Badia

'I pass behind the palazzo with its crenellated tower and one-handed clock': Palazzo Vecchio at night.

and the Palazzo Vecchio were already standing. So too was the little church of Santa Margherita de Cerchi, otherwise known as Dante's Church, where his family prayed and where Beatrice, the great love of his life, is remembered daily by fresh flowers placed on her family tomb.

All these places feature prominently in Dan Brown's *Inferno*, which is saturated with descriptions of Florence as well as references to Dante and the books of his *Divine Comedy*. With irony, Dan Brown has made his anti-hero Bertrand Zobrist a Dante aficionado, a man who seems to have entirely entered into the poet's *Inferno*, seeking his way to Paradise through Hell, and finding his muse, his blessed Beatrice, in Sienna Brooks.

VISIONS OF HELL

Not surprisingly, a fair amount is said about hell in Dan Brown's *Inferno*, which lends a significant atmosphere of dread to the thriller. The novel makes some pretty big claims, however, concerning Dante's contribution to the image of hell, not only in medieval times, but still to this day. In a lecture that Robert Langdon gives to the Società Dante Alighieri in Vienna, for example, he tells his audience that 'Dante's *Inferno* created a world of pain and suffering beyond all previous human imagination, and his writing quite literally defined our modern visions of hell.' And then comes Dan Brown's trademark kick against the Catholic Church. 'And believe me,' Langdon continues in his lecture, 'the Catholic Church has much to thank Dante for. His *Inferno* terrified the faithful for centuries, and no doubt tripled church attendance among the fearful.'

But this is not correct. Neither Dante nor the Catholic Church invented hell or fire or other torments. Ancient Egyptian religion, for example, featured the Weighing of the Heart ritual, in which the heart of the dead person was weighed against the feather of Maat. If found wanting, it was immediately devoured by a female demon called Ammut who stood by a lake of fire – or sometimes the heart was thrown directly into the lake. Nor was that the end of it; the devoured soul, or the soul thrown into the fiery lake, remained in restless torment for all time, a state known as the second death. Exactly this image of the fiery lake found its way into early Christianity, appearing in Revelation, where everyone from pagans to Roman emperors is hurled into a lake of burning fire.

In fact Robert Langdon saw a horrific scene of hell, depicting Satan tearing and devouring the souls of dead sinners, in the ceiling mosaic of the Baptistery in Florence. As a professor of religious art and symbology, he should have known that the

The ancient Egyptian Weighing of the Heart ritual; the female demon Ammut, a four-legged beast of destruction, crouches patiently at the right.

mosaic was done in the early thirteenth century, about forty years before Dante was born.

There is hell in Islam too; in the Koran it goes under several names, including 'a fire whose fuel is stones and men', or simply 'the fire', 'burning', 'scorching fire' and 'crushing pressure'. So fearsome is the notion of hell in Islam that even its utterance in speech is taken as a dreadful omen.

Hell gets big play in Dan Brown's *Inferno* in the way it is used to portray an overpopulated world at some point in the near future, a world that some people are certain will collapse for lack of resources. This is illustrated by Sienna Brooks recalling her traumatic youthful visit to Manila, the capital of the Philippines, which she describes in chapter 79 as 'passing through the gates of hell':

> *Manila had six-hour traffic jams, suffocating pollution, and a horrifying sex trade, whose workers consisted primarily of young children, many of whom had been sold to pimps by parents who took solace in knowing that at least their children would be fed. ... All around her, she could see humanity overrun by its primal instinct for survival. When they face desperation ... human beings become animals.'*

It's true that the Philippines have a very high growth rate, albeit one that has almost halved in the last few years. Pakistan has a far higher growth rate, as does the whole of the largely Muslim Middle East. Nigeria has the highest growth rate of all; its population is about half Muslim and half Christian, with Catholics representing about a quarter of all Christians, which is to say about an eighth of the country's total population. Which makes one wonder why the Philippines are singled out for mention in *Inferno*. And then one remembers: this is one of only two Catholic majority countries in Asia (the other being East Timor). So is it the growth rate that Dan Brown is objecting to, or is it the Catholicism?

It does look that way when you consider the exchange that takes place in chapter 22 of *Inferno* between Elizabeth Sinskey, director of the World Health Organisation, and Bertrand Zobrist, the cull-minded geneticist. He is accusing the WHO of doing nothing about controlling population, but she objects: 'Recently we spent millions of dollars sending doctors into Africa to deliver free condoms and educate people about birth control'. To which Zobrist replies, 'And an even bigger army of Catholic missionaries marched in on your heels and told the Africans that if they used the condoms, they'd all go to hell'.

Even if that were true, Catholics are a minority in Africa, where Islam is the largest religion, and most Christians are Protestants. To hang population growth on armies of condom-damning Catholic missionaries does not make mathematical sense.

Nevertheless, Bertrand Zobrist, the man who wants to thin the human herd, is an optimist. He says that we have learned from Dante that we have to pass through Hell to reach Paradise. There again, Zobrist does not have his facts straight. Dante makes it plain that no one leaves Hell – or rather none but those Old Testament Jews who were carried aloft by Jesus after the crucifixion when he harrowed Hell, and Dante and Virgil themselves, who being poets could get away with almost anything. Otherwise, as Dante makes clear, Hell is not a remedial state; it is utter and eternal damnation. Dan Brown adds to the confusion at the very start of his book when he states as 'FACT' that Dante's underworld is 'populated by entities known as "shades" – bodiless souls trapped between life and death'. In Dante's Hell they are not trapped between life and death; they are totally and forever dead.

One other curiosity is worth mentioning about hell in Dan Brown's *Inferno*, and that concerns the epigraph, words that are repeated several times throughout the book: 'The darkest places in hell are reserved for those who maintain their neutrality in times of moral crisis'. Although the epigraph offers no source, those words are described in chapter 38 as 'a famous quote derived from the work of Dante Alighieri'.

Dante never said any such thing. The quote is in fact derived from a remark by President John F Kennedy: 'Dante once said that the hottest places in hell are reserved for those who in a period of moral crisis maintain their neutrality'. Kennedy, for his part, was either making it up – he liked to come up with 'literary' quotations – or he misremembered what Dante

Devils at play – one of Gustave Doré's illustrations for the classic nineteenth-century edition of Dante's Divine Comedy *(1861).*

really said in Canto III of the *Inferno* about the cowards and the opportunists:

> *This wretched state is borne by the wretched souls of those who lived without disgrace and without praise … who were not rebels, nor faithful to God, but were for themselves. … They have no hope of death, and so abject is their blind life that they are envious of every other lot. The world suffers no report of them to live. Pity and justice despise them. Let us not talk of them.*

In other words, they are contemptible. Whatever Dan Brown may suggest, however, they are not in the darkest place in

Hell. Instead they are right at the top, just inside the gate, even better off than the virtuous pagans who inhabit Limbo a bit further down.

THE BIG ISSUES

> *I talked to a lot of scientists who are also concerned about it and I came to understand that overpopulation is the issue to which all of our other environmental issues are tied ... things like ozone, where do we get our clean water, starvation, deforestation. These we consider problems. But they're really symptoms of overpopulation. So overpopulation to me seems like the big issue.*
>
> Dan Brown, *BBC interview*

Bertrand Zobrist fascinates Brown, who wonders whether it's a madman that he's created, or a genius. 'There are moments in the novel, or at least when I was writing it, when I thought, wow, Zobrist may save the world here. Maybe this is how far we have to go to stop this.'

Brown says that he has three watchwords for anyone reading his *Inferno*. Contrapasso, that is letting the punishment suit the sin; Malthusianism, the notion that the human population can only forever get bigger until it is slashed by disease, famine or war; and Transhumanism, which calls for the manipulation of our own genetic make-up to create posthumans. As discussed in Chapter Nine of this book, Transhumanism may be a science, or it may have more to do with the cult of self and paranoia – or with the eugenics so beloved of Swedes and Nazis. The word Transhumanism deliberately, and perhaps naively or cynically, harks back to humanism, the great movement that, with its valuing of human curiosity and desire to improve the human lot, lay at the heart of the Renaissance.

Although Dan Brown himself says 'I don't know' and 'I don't have an answer', disavowing any suggestion that he's actually advocating an extreme solution of questionable science and morality, a great many readers and reviewers of his *Inferno* have finished the book believing that both Brown and his hero Robert Langdon go along with Bertrand Zobrist in accepting the need for a modern-day plague. Not a Black Death, perhaps, causing physical pain and immediate death, and leaving bodies rotting in the streets, but a plague that has the same end effect, of scything away a third of the human population and of stealing millions of futures.

PART ONE

DANTE
AND HIS WORLD

✳ CHAPTER ONE ✳

𝔇ante 𝔄lighieri

D ante Alighieri was born in 1265 in Florence and died in exile in Ravenna in 1321 at about the age of fifty-six. What we know of his life comes from his own writings, principally the *Vita Nuova*, his autobiography, or psychobiography, of his youth, begun in 1293, and his *Divine Comedy*. He started to write the *Inferno*, the first section of the latter, in 1308, although its narrative actually begins as the night before Good Friday 1300.

Dante also had two early biographers. The first was Giovanni Boccaccio (1313–75), famous as the author of the *Decameron*, who tracked down people who had memories of Dante or who had stories passed down to them, among them Dante's own daughter whom Boccaccio met in Ravenna. The second was Leonardo Bruni (1370–1444), regarded as the first modern historian, who came on the scene much later but felt that Boccaccio had concentrated too much on the romantic side of Dante – 'love and sighs and burning tears' – at the expense of 'the memorable things'.

Though Dante was very proud of his ancestry, which he said went back to Roman times, there is no evidence that he could trace his family beyond his great-great-grandfather, a knight called Cacciaguida degli Elisei, whom he mentions in Canto XV of his *Paradiso*, and was born no earlier than 1100. Cacciaguida's son took the name Alighieri from his mother's family, and his descendants continued to live in Florence, where Dante was born in 1265 to Alighiero di Bellincione and his wife Bella.

MINOR ARISTOCRACY

The Alighieri were minor aristocracy. They did not rank among the *magnati*, the magnates, who ruled Florence until a year after Dante's birth when the Ghibellines, the faction representing the nobles and their allies the Holy Roman Empire, were overthrown and the city became Europe's first democracy since the Roman republic. The Alighieri family, who supported the Guelfs, the faction allied to the Pope in Rome, owned several small estates in the countryside nearby, but as the rents from their land were not enough to support them, they also relied on commerce and trade. Records show that Dante and his brother made something of a living by buying and selling property, and also busied themselves arranging the necessary loans and negotiating interest and repayments.

Plaque in the Florentine quarter where Dante 'was born and grew up on the fair stream of the Arno, in the great city'.

In this way the Alighieris, part aristocrats and part merchant family, reflected the character of Florence itself, a city in which the nobility and the merchants lived uncomfortably side by side, each competing for dominance but needing the other. The aristocracy provided the protective military might, the merchants the financial prosperity of the city.

Within Dante's lifetime the conflicts between factions – aristocracy versus the growing power of the merchant guilds, Ghibellines versus Guelfs, and Blacks versus Whites – brought terrible strife to Florence and would lead to his exile from his beloved city.

Dante's mother dreams of his birth

According to Boccaccio, who collected the story – perhaps from Dante's daughter – Dante's mother Bella had a dream during her pregnancy about the child to whom she was soon to give birth. Bella dreamed that she was lying in a green meadow under a lofty laurel tree by a clear stream when she gave birth to a son who grew into a shepherd, feeding himself only on the berries from the laurel tree and the waters of the stream. He strove with all his power to have the leaves of the laurel tree whose fruit had nourished him, but he seemed to fall, and when he rose again he was no longer a man but had become a peacock.

The laurel symbolises immortality, and its leaves have traditionally been used to crown men of great achievement, heroes and athletes and poets; it also symbolises hidden knowledge. In classical and Christian tradition the peacock likewise symbolises the cycle of the sun and therefore immortality, while its tail symbolises the starry sky. Peacocks were also used in medieval art as signs of eternal bliss and of the beatific vision of the soul when it comes face to face with God, while in esoteric tradition peacocks symbolise wholeness – a fitting symbol for Dante, whose life would attempt to straddle a divided world and whose greatest yearning was for wholeness.

Neither Bella nor anyone else understood the meaning of the dream, but soon after, when she gave birth to a son, she named him Dante, meaning Giver. And, in due course, he proved worthy of the name; Boccaccio observed that by writing in the vernacular, in the Tuscan dialect of common Italian rather than in Latin, he opened the way for the return of the Muses and brought dead poetry back to life, so that 'he could not rightly have borne any other name but Dante'.

THE MAKING OF A POET

Dante's mother died in 1270, when he was only five. His father, who soon remarried, arranged for the boy to be educated in the liberal arts, studying history and philosophy, mathematics and classical literature. When Dante's father died in 1280, Brunetto Latini became Dante's guardian and responsible for his education. A considerable philosopher and rhetorician, Latini knew both how to speak well and how to write well, and served in many high positions in the government of Florence. Dante would write Latini into his *Inferno* at Canto XV, saying that by teaching Dante how to write, 'You taught me how man makes himself immortal'. For all that, Latini is in the third ring of the Seventh Circle of Hell, where the sinners of violence against nature go: Latini is a homosexual and the Church condemns him as a sodomite to the burning plain beneath the forever falling fiery rain. But Dante feels differently: if it were up to him, 'you had not yet been banished from humanity'. Under Latini's guidance, Dante's education advanced, and he further developed his close knowledge of the Latin poets, among them Ovid, Horace and especially Virgil.

For all the seriousness of his studies, however, Dante never cut himself off from the world; he moved easily about

Florence with friends his own age. For Boccaccio it is almost inconceivable that young men could be interested in women other than carnally, and yet, he admits, Dante's was a chaste love. Leonardo Bruni agrees: 'He consorted in his youth with amorous swains, and was himself too engaged in the passion, not by way of lustfulness but in gentleness of heart.' Soon he was composing his first sonnets, and in 1284 he joined the group of poets known as the Fedeli d'Amore, the Faithful Followers of Love. These poets have been described as rare spirits trying to introduce nobility to life – retaining something of the chivalry associated with the overturned aristocracy of Florence, the courtly poetry of France and the songs of the troubadours. But they began, as it were, with raw material. Their aim was to turn their experiences with women into erotic and mystical poetry.

MARRIAGE AND LOVE

Families were the building blocks of political and economic relationships in Florentine society, and arranged marriages at a very young age were common. In about 1277, when Dante was still only eleven, his father arranged an advantageous marriage to Gemma Donati, daughter of Manetto Donati, who as a member of the powerful Donati family would bring with her a dowry. He married her eight years later, in 1285, when he was twenty; they had three sons, Jacopo, Pietro and Giovanni, and a daughter called Antonia. Boccaccio did not think much of the marriage, writing: 'We may think what miseries these rooms hide, which from outside are reputed places of delight to those without eyes which can pierce through walls'. But then Boccaccio did not approve of any marriage, especially as he himself had been bound by a marriage contract at the age of one, and as he admits he had no idea whether Dante's was a

Gustave Doré's portrait of Dante Alighieri wearing the laurel crown.

happy marriage or not. But Boccaccio does say that once Dante was exiled from Florence he would never go where Gemma was, nor would he allow her to come to him. And we also know that Dante never once mentioned his wife's name in anything he wrote. Even before Dante's marriage to Gemma was arranged, however, he had fallen in love with Beatrice Portinari. Dante was nine, she was eight; the occasion was a

May Day party at her father's house nearby. Beatrice became the love of his life; his poetry was devoted to her. She too was spoken for in an arranged marriage, and Dante hardly ever did more than gain glimpses of her from afar, but when she died at the age of twenty-four he was devastated.

In a later prose work, the *Convivio*, Dante wrote that the young are overcome by supor, an astonishment of the mind, when they encounter something that brings awareness of great and wonderful things. The consequence of supor is a sense of reverence and a desire to know more, and that is what happened to Dante upon first seeing his Florentine girl. For the rest of his life, all his work, one way or another, served to augment that worship and increase that knowledge.

When Dante is lost in the dark wood, Beatrice sends Virgil to show him the way, and when Dante has braved the horrors of Hell, Beatrice is waiting for him in Purgatory to lead him into the highest realms of Paradise. Dante's love for Beatrice would be his reason for living; his passion for her was shared only with his passion for politics, and this too would lead him to write his *Divine Comedy*.

WAR AND POLITICS

If his studies were arduous, his marriage passionless, and his love for Beatrice ethereal, Dante was nevertheless a robust young man, ready to go to battle for his city and eager to enter into its politics. In 1289 he fought with the Florentines on the side of the Guelfs in the battle of Campaldino against the Ghibelline forces of Arezzo. The Florentines and their allies raised a rabble of ten thousand soldiers on foot but also something like two thousand mounted men, with Dante riding among the cavalry. An overwhelming Florentine victory, the battle guaranteed Guelf rule in the city. But in a first extreme reaction to the Ghibelline defeat the Florentines excluded all citizens of noble birth from public office, though this stern measure was relaxed provided the intending candidate obtained nominal membership of one of the guilds.

The guilds of Florence – the cloth merchants, wool merchants, bankers, doctors and apothecaries and so on – were more than trade associations; they had become self-regulating political institutions governed by an elected committee of priors. Each guild also had its own armed enforcers headed by a captain of the guards, just as the aristocrats had theirs. In addition, as explained on p.99, new Black and White factions arose within the victorious Guelfs themselves. The former wished to keep Florence close to the papacy, the latter opposed papal influence and particularly that of Pope Boniface VIII. All of which may have suggested to Dan Brown the myriad security forces that appear bewilderingly in the pages of his *Inferno.*

Aristocratic rule had often been capricious, whereas merchants required stability to flourish. For the Florentine republic, that made it essential to maintain an equilibrium between the two great powers who wielded influence in northern Italy at the time: the Holy Roman Empire, whose king was based in Germany, and the Church and pope at Rome. For Dante these were the two suns, as he called them, one representing secular rule, the other spiritual. Keeping them in balance ensured the greatest independence and stability for Florence, and seemed to Dante to bring harmony to the world. His aim was to achieve harmony too among the factions in Florence, between the nobles and the 'people' as members of the artisan and merchant guilds were called, and between the Blacks and the Whites.

In 1295 Dante entered the doctors' and apothecaries' guild, one of the city's seven major guilds. In the ensuing years, the records show Dante speaking and voting in various councils of

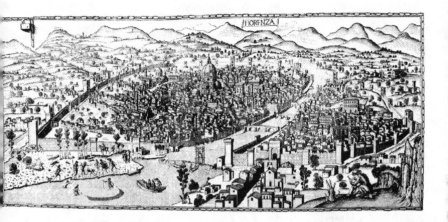

A woodcut of Florence from Boccaccio's Life of Dante.

the Florentine republic; and in 1300 he was elected to the city's highest office as one of the six chief executive priors of Florence.

Following an outbreak of factional strife between the Blacks and the Whites, Dante led the priors in taking the drastic measure of banishing the chief figures among both factions. One of these was Dante's friend and fellow poet in the Fedeli d'Amore, Guido Cavalcanti, who was a leader of the Whites.

But Pope Boniface VIII was eager for a showdown with the Whites in Florence, along with other anti-Church factions elsewhere in Tuscany. He called upon Charles of Valois, a brother of Philip the Fair, the king of France, to lead an army into Italy. To avert an armed intervention, the government of Florence sent Dante to Rome as an envoy to the pope, where Boniface toyed with him, keeping him delayed in the city for three months towards the end of 1301. Meanwhile, behind his back, the Blacks were being helped to power in Florence by the French mediator to whom they had opened the city gates.

Only the year before, Boniface had declared 1300 a jubilee, marking thirteen hundred years since the birth of Christ. To all Christians who made the pilgrimage to St Peter's in Rome he promised full remission of their sins – at vast profit to the Vatican – even as he sat on the throne of Constantine the Great, where holding the symbols of temporal dominion, the sword, the sceptre and the crown, he called to the crowd, 'I am Caesar!' Outraged by the machinations of the pope, Dante became one of the most outspoken critics of Boniface and would consign him to the Eighth Circle of Hell for simony.

UNDER SENTENCE OF DEATH

It is no coincidence that Dante set his *Divine Comedy* in 1300, for in a sense that year became his own jubilee, in which he lost his way in the dark wood of worldly error and began his journey to personal salvation. Though he had reached the apogee of Florentine politics when he became one of its six ruling priors, the harmony he had hoped to bring to his native city turned to dust. His friend Guido Cavalcanti died of malaria during the banishment into which he had been sent by Dante himself. And in the following year, during his embassy to Rome, Dante was outwitted by the pope and Florence fell into the hands of his enemies, the Blacks. Dante never saw Florence again.

At the start of 1302, while Dante was still in Rome, he was condemned by the triumphant Blacks to pay a fine of five thousand florins and to be banished from Florence for two years. Behind the legalities it was in effect a political purge that was determined to break him and make him submit. Two months later, when he refused to pay and by implication admit to the charge of graft levelled against him, the banishment was made permanent. The stipulation was added that should he ever be caught within the territory of Florence he would be burned alive at the stake.

YEARS OF EXILE

In exile Dante became, in his own words, 'a Florentine by birth but not in spirit'; instead he joined those 'to whom the world is our native country, just as the sea is to the fish'. As he wrote in a later prose work, the *Convivio*:

> *After it was the pleasure of the citizens of that fairest and most famous daughter of Rome, Florence, to cast me out of her dearest bosom, I have wandered through almost every region to which this tongue of ours extends, a stranger, almost a beggar, exposing to view against my will the stroke of fortune which is often wont unjustly to be charged to the account of the stricken. Truly I have been a ship without sail and without rudder, wafted to divers havens and inlets and shores, by the parching wind which woeful poverty exhales.'*

Time and again in the years that followed, Dante was offered the chance to return to Florence, but only if he made a public atonement. If he would come to the Baptistery dressed in sackcloth and submit to a ritual humiliation, he would be accepted back into the city. Proudly, the poet refused, saying that if he returned at all he would stand before his baptismal font only to accept the poet's laurel crown. His final answer came in these lines from the *Paradiso*, Canto XXV 1–9:

> *If it ever come to pass that the sacred poem*
> *to which both heaven and earth have set their hand*
> *so as to have made me lean for many years*
> *should overcome the cruelty that bars me*
> *from the fair sheepfold where I slept as a lamb,*
> *an enemy to the wolves that make war on it,*
> *with another voice now and other fleece*

I shall return a poet and at the font
of my baptism take the laurel crown.

DANTE AND THE TEMPLARS

Dante's poetry did not, however, serve him as a passport. For two decades he led the wandering life of a learned courtier, travelling throughout northern Italy, to France, and according to Boccaccio as far north as Paris.

Quite possibly he was in Paris on Friday 13 October 1307, the day king Philip IV, the Fair, launched a nationwide dawn raid against the Knights Templar, arresting everyone associated with the order and putting them on trial for blasphemy, heresy, sodomy and a host of other charges that were designed to smear their reputation forever.

It has been suggested that Dante himself had had some connection with the order in his youth, for the Templars had a house in Florence. Whatever the truth of that, Dante was outraged at their arrest, which he ascribed to simple theft by the French king who wanted the Templars' money. Writing in the *Purgatorio*, Canto XX, Dante described Philip as another Pontius Pilate who 'ruthless' and 'without law ... bears into the Temple his greedy sails'.

WRITING THE INFERNO

Dante came to rest for a while in Verona, the guest of Can Grande Della Scala, who was the leader of the Ghibelline League; Dante's politics had now swung from his youthful support of the Guelfs, who had since betrayed him, to the Ghibellines. There at Della Scala's sophisticated court, and with access to one of the best libraries in Europe, Dante began the *Inferno* in 1308. He also lived briefly in Bologna and Padua. His powerful and aristocratic

The Casa di Dante museum in the poet's native quarter of Florence.

hosts might use him to compose in Latin elaborate despatches or treaties with a neighbouring city, and sometimes they sent him on diplomatic missions. But in his lack of independence he learned 'how bitter another's bread is'.

Dante spent his last years at Ravenna, in the house of its ruler, Guido Novello da Polenta. Guido was a nephew of Francesca da Rimini, who had been murdered by her husband in around 1286, following an adulterous affair. Dante had already written Francesca into his *Inferno*, placing her along with her lover in the Second Circle of Hell. By this time, it seems, Dante was sufficiently famous that to have a lustful aunt celebrated by the great poet was something to be proud of. Her fame was to grow still further; the original name of Rodin's *The Kiss* was *Francesca da Rimini*.

RETURN TO HIS STARS

In the house of Francesca's nephew, Dante completed his *Divine Comedy*, ascending to Paradise with Beatrice and beholding the face of God. He had with him one of his sons and his daughter Antonia, who had become a nun and had taken the name Beatrice.

Not long afterwards, Dante was sent by Guido on a diplomatic mission to Venice. He chose rather than to return in comfort by boat along the coast to travel through the marshland of the estuary of the River Po, and contracted malaria, the same illness that had killed the great friend of his youth, Guido Cavalcanti. Dante died in Ravenna; the exact date is disputed, but tradition places his death at the Feast of the Exaltation of the Holy Cross, 14 September 1321. An epitaph was composed: 'Ungrateful Florence, a cruel fatherland, rewarded her bard with the bitter fruit of exile; but compassionate Ravenna is glad to have received him in the bosom of Guido Novello, its revered leader. In the year of Our Lord, one thousand three hundred and thrice seven, on the ides of September, then did he return to his stars'.

Dante was given a stately funeral and his dead brow was adorned with a laurel crown. But the magnificent tomb intended for the poet was never built; Guido da Polenta was overthrown exactly a year later, and Dante rests in a modest mausoleum. Florence has ever since tried to have his bones, but Ravenna has refused.

✳ CHAPTER TWO ✳

𝕭eatrice

W hen Dante has lost his way in life and is stumbling about in the dark forest, the Roman poet Virgil comes to show him the way – that is how the *Inferno*, the first book of the *Divine Comedy*, begins. But before they can get out, they have to go down, into the very depths of Hell. Virgil is a denizen of Limbo, that place where virtuous pagans born before the advent of Christ remain suspended for eternity. Nevertheless Virgil has had thirteen hundred years to kill; he has done some exploring underground, and knows his way around. He is also a celebrity, 'of whom the fame still in the world endures, / And shall endure, long-lasting as the world'. These words are spoken by a beautiful woman, her eyes shining brighter than the stars, who visits Virgil in Limbo and implores his help. She is Beatrice, who is dwelling in Paradise, but who has seen Dante's plight and wants to save him before it is too late. 'Love moved me', she says.

BEATRICE OF PARADISE

Beatrice is the love of Dante's life, a radiant creature with emerald eyes, a voice 'gentle and low', and a motherly smile, who died when she was twenty-four. Dante, who is now thirty-five, in the middle of his life, has not seen Beatrice for more than ten years and he does not see her now. Instead first he must follow Virgil through the Inferno, then upwards to the summit of Purgatory where Beatrice appears to him and then shows him the way to Paradise where she takes her place in the highest tier, two seats away from the Virgin Mary.

This is an ethereal Beatrice; Dante has turned the flesh-and-blood woman that he knew into an angel, though he had begun doing that already when she was alive. In fact there is some question about whether Beatrice was ever real, though Dante's experience of her, which he describes in his *Vita Nuova*, is so wacky that oddly her reality becomes all the more believable.

THE GIRL NEXT DOOR

Dante began composing the *Divine Comedy* in his mid-thirties, but Beatrice makes her first appearance before that, in his autobiographical work called *Vita Nuova* (New Life), a prose account of his younger years, which includes a number of poems as well, and which he wrote in his mid-twenties. Dante writes that Beatrice 'appeared to me at the beginning of her ninth year almost, and I saw her almost at the end of my ninth year' (Dante would forever identify the number nine with Beatrice). Though both were only children, Dante fell in love with her instantly on that May day in 1274, and his love for her continued to burn with extraordinary intensity well beyond the day she died at the age of twenty-four in 1290. From the moment he saw Beatrice, he became a man possessed by a divine power, by Love itself.

> *At that moment, I say most truly that the spirit*
> *of life, which hath its dwelling in the secretest*
> *chamber of the heart, began to tremble so violently*

that the least pulses of my body shook therewith; and in trembling it said these words: 'Here is a deity stronger than I; who, coming, shall rule over me'.

According to Giovanni Boccaccio, famous as the author of the ribald tales called *The Decameron*, who lived almost a lifetime after Dante and was the first to write his biography, this meeting between Dante and Beatrice took place at the house of Folco Portinari. A wealthy banker and philanthropist of Florence, Portinari had invited friends and neighbours to celebrate the first of May. The house is today the Palazzo Portinari Salviati at 6 Via del Corso, very close to where Dante himself lived. Dante came along with his father, and here he

Henry Holiday's Pre-Raphaelite painting of Dante's encounter with Beatrice as she walks past the Santa Trinità Bridge. Beatrice, in the white dress, is accompanied by her friend Monna Vanna, and her maidservant.

mingled with other children, girls and boys, of his own age. In Boccaccio's words:

> There was among the crowd of children a little daughter of the aforesaid Folco, whose name was Bice (although he always called her by her full name, that is, Beatrice), who was perhaps eight years old, very comely – for her age – and very gentle and pleasing in her actions, with ways and words more serious and modest than her youth required; and besides this, with features very delicate and well formed, and, further, so full of beauty and of sweet winsomeness that she was declared by many to be like a little angel. She, then – such as I paint her and perhaps even more beautiful – appeared at this feast to the eyes of our Dante – not, I believe, for the first time, but for the first time with power to enamour him. And although a mere boy, he received her sweet image in his heart with such affection that from that day forward it never departed thence while he lived.

BEATRICE EATS DANTE'S HEART

As Dante grew older his passion for Beatrice increased. He could find no pleasure or peace except by seeing her, going wherever he thought he might again glimpse her eyes, her face. 'Oh, senseless judgment of lovers!', Boccaccio writes. 'Who else but they would think by adding to the fuel to make the flames less?' But it was always a chaste love, Boccaccio is sure. Having studied Dante's writings and those of his friends, and interviewing people in Florence whose families may have known him, Boccaccio concluded that 'his love was most virtuous, nor did there ever appear, by look or word or sign, any wanton appetite either in the lover or in her whom he loved'.

Boccaccio, who knew and wrote about carnal desire, remarked that 'this is no small marvel to the world of today, from which all virtuous pleasure has so fled, and which is so accustomed to having whatever pleases it conform to its lust'.

There must have been numerous sightings of Beatrice, many encounters in the streets of Florence, but Dante makes no mention of any of this; if they happened they happened silently, no words passed between them. Instead the next great moment, he writes in the *Vita Nuova*, came 'nine years exactly' after they met at her father's May Day party. Beatrice, 'dressed all in pure white', was walking along a street (he does not name the street) in the company of two older women. The hour was 'the ninth of the day' (three o'clock in the afternoon) and she stopped and greeted him; 'it was the first time that any words from her reached my ears'. Overwhelmed and intoxicated, he stumbled to his room.

There he fell asleep and was seized by a vision, a cloud of fire, and emerging from it the figure of a man, the Lord of Love, frightening to behold yet filled with joy. 'I am your master', he said. In his arms Dante noticed a woman, naked except for a loosely wrapped crimson cloth, and recognised her as Beatrice. And in his hand was a fiery object, which he held before Dante saying, 'Behold your heart'. Then he pressed it upon Beatrice, who ate it. Still carrying Beatrice in his arms, the Lord of Love ascended, as though to heaven, and Dante awoke with a start, realising that this vision had come to him at 'the fourth hour (which is to say, the first of the nine last hours) of the night'.

Afterwards Dante wrote a sonnet about his vision, which he sent to Guido Cavalcanti, leader of the Fedeli d'Amore, the Faithful Followers of Love, a group of poets of erotic and mystical inclinations. He was soon invited to become a member.

EMERALD EYES

The next time Dante speaks of seeing Beatrice, it is in a church. He does not say which church, but the church of Santa Margherita de Cerchi in a passageway off the Via del Corso was the parish church of the Dante family, and also the burial place of members of the Portinari family – in fact it claims to hold the tomb of Beatrice herself. The occasion is a mass, and prayers are being said to the Virgin Mary. Dante has taken a place that gives him a clear view of Beatrice, his 'beatitude'. He stares at her so intently that another woman, in the direct line of sight between Beatrice and himself, keeps turning round, fancying that he is looking at her, and when the mass is over sure enough he hears worshippers remarking on his attraction to this woman. That gives him the idea that he can hide his adoration of Beatrice by pretending to be in love with this other woman, 'a screen to the truth' as he calls her. So well did he play his part that people who had noted his lovelorn behaviour now thought they had discovered its cause. To complete the deception, Dante wrote numerous poems in honour of this 'screen lady', and thereby concealed the truth of his love for Beatrice for many years.

During all of this, as we follow his life in the pages of the *Vita Nuova*, Dante never offers a description of Beatrice. He says

nothing about the colour of her eyes, the colour of her hair, the complexion of her skin, nothing of her figure or the way she walks, nor does he mention that she is betrothed to another man whom she eventually marries in 1287 at the age of twenty-one, nor that he has been betrothed from the age of eleven, and that he marries before Beatrice, when he is twenty in 1285. Neither does he have anything more to say about the physical Beatrice in the whole of the *Divine Comedy*, other than a single reference to her emerald eyes.

BEATRICE CUTS DANTE DEAD

As it happened, the screen lady left Florence at about the same time as Dante himself had to travel in the same direction. Soon the rumour went round that he and the lady were having an affair. When the rumour reached Beatrice – that 'destroyer of all evil and the queen of all good', who 'alone was my blessedness' – she passed him in the street and cut him dead.

The effect on Dante was devastating. Until then, he says, his anticipation of seeing Beatrice again and receiving her greeting so filled him with love that no man was his enemy: 'I would have pardoned whosoever had done me an injury'. Withdrawing to his room in pain and confusion, he was revisited by his vision of the Lord of Love who wept for Dante, explaining 'I am as the centre of a circle, to the which all parts of the circumference bear an equal relation, but with thee it is not thus'. Dante does not understand, and asks, 'What thing is this, Master, that thou hast spoken thus darkly?' To which the Lord of Love answers, 'Demand no more than may be useful to thee'.

The implication is that not being at the centre of the circle is a bad thing, but Dante has not yet undergone sufficient spiritual development to understand why. The reader, however, can look ahead to the *Divine Comedy*, which was then still to be written. There we see that circles describe Dante's conception of the universe. The circles of the *Inferno* lead down to the deepest pit of Hell, the circular terraces of the *Purgatorio* ascend to the sky, and the spheres of the *Paradiso* – spheres being the three-dimensional version of circles – expand beyond the boundaries of this earth, sphere encompassed by sphere, and encompassed again by greater and greater spheres, until a vast sphere encompasses the entire universe beyond which is nothing but the all-encompassing mind of God.

The Lord of Love is saying to Dante that he must stand at the centre, which means to love not just a woman but the whole universe. Already in the *Vita Nuova* this begins to happen – which is why Dante calls it the New Life – and the process will reach its fruition in the *Divine Comedy* where through his love for Beatrice he journeys into the Inferno, through Purgatory, and emerges into Paradise, driven by his growing understanding that his love for Beatrice is one and the same as the divine love that is the motive force throughout all creation.

DEATH OF BEATRICE

Meanwhile, in the *Vita Nuova*, the death of Beatrice's father in 1289 leads Dante to reflect on her own mortality.

> *And then perceiving how frail a thing life is, even though health keep with it, the matter seemed to me so pitiful that I could not choose but weep; and weeping I said within myself: 'Certainly it must some time come to pass that the very gentle Beatrice will die'. Then, feeling bewildered, I closed mine eyes; and my brain began to be in travail as the brain of one frantic.*

Dante's fears would come true soon enough. He had begun to write a poem about his love for Beatrice and how he craved her greeting – 'Always soliciting / My lady's salutation piteously' – when he learned that she had died. These words from the Lamentations of Jeremiah 1:1 came to him: 'How doth the city sit solitary, that was full of people! How is she become as a widow, she that was great among the nations!' Otherwise he was all but struck dumb with grief: 'My pen doth not suffice to write in a fit manner of this thing'. Instead it is left to Boccaccio to describe what Dante could not bear to write in the *Vita Nuova*:

> The beautiful Beatrice was nearly at the end of her twenty-fourth year, when, as pleased Him who is all-powerful, she left the anguish of this world and departed to the glory which her own merits had prepared for her. At her departure Dante was left in such sorrow, grief, and tears that many of those nearest him, both relatives and friends, believed there would be no other end to them except his death; and this they thought must come quickly, seeing that he gave ear to no comfort or consolation offered him. The days were like the nights and the nights the days; and no hour of either passed without cries and sighs and a great quantity of tears. His eyes seemed two copious fountains of flowing water, so that most marvelled whence he acquired enough moisture to supply his weeping. ...
>
> He was, by his weeping and the pain that his heart felt within him, and by his taking no care of himself, become outwardly almost a wild thing to look upon, lean, unshaven, and almost completely transformed from what he had been wont to be before.

THE MYSTIC NUMBER NINE

How Beatrice died is not known, but it was probably in childbirth. Dante composed himself sufficiently to write two pages about the number nine in relation to her death:

The number nine, which number hath often had mention in what hath gone before, (and not, as it might appear, without reason), seems also to have borne a part in the manner of her death: it is therefore right that I should say somewhat thereof.' For Dante nine is the number of Beatrice, the square of three which is the Trinity, the Father, the Son and the Holy Spirit; nine is also the number of Love.

WAS BEATRICE REAL?

But the question arises, was Beatrice ever real? Though the *Divine Comedy* is populated with historical figures like Cleopatra, the prophet Mohammed and several popes, it is

The tomb of Beatrice. As Dan Brown describes, the wicker basket alongside holds handwritten letters from lovelorn visitors.

nevertheless a fiction; Dante did not really venture into Hell. And so why believe that the Beatrice sitting two seats away from the Virgin Mary confirms the existence of Beatrice Portinari or any other real young woman of Florence?

The *Vita Nuova*, however, is a different matter. This book is presented by Dante as a memoir, a selection of memories:

> *In that part of the book of my memory before the which is little that can be read, there is a rubric, saying, Incipit Vita Nova* [here begins a new life]. *Under such rubric I find written many things; and among them the words which I purpose to copy into this little book; if not all of them, at the least their substance.*

Here, before Dante wrote the *Divine Comedy*, is where a Florentine woman called Beatrice makes her appearance. Not that Dante tells us much about her other than her first name and age and death. We will just have to take his word for it that he is not making her up – not that he even gives us his word for that.

THE BEATRICE MYSTERY

The evidence for the existence of Beatrice depends on three things. The first is Dante's description of her and his reaction to her; one has to decide if it rings true. Most people reading the *Vita Nuova* do feel that in all its extreme sensibility the portrait of the lovelorn young Dante is believable. But the girl could be anyone, and the name Beatrice could just be a cover. After all, Beatrice means blessed, which is how Dante describes her and deploys her from the start of the *Vita Nuova* to the end of the *Divine Comedy*. Beatrice is a name, a quality, that Dante could have applied to any Giovanna or Maria.

The second piece of evidence comes from Boccaccio, who was born in 1313, eight years before Dante's death, and who probably wrote his life of the poet after 1350, the year in which he is known to have visited Dante's daughter, who took the name Beatrice when she became a nun. That visit was part of Boccaccio's researches into his subject, which included interviewing anyone he could find who actually remembered the poet or whose family had some connection – which in the case of verifying the events of the *Vita Nuova* meant reaching back sixty years and more. And so it is to Boccaccio that we owe the information that there really was a Beatrice, that she was the daughter of Folco Portinari, and that Dante met her at a May Day party at the Portinari house. Although what Boccaccio actually says is that the girl was called Bice, which is generally used as the diminutive for Beatrice.

What led Boccaccio to identify Dante's Beatrice with Folco Portinari's daughter? We are not told. Dante was not popular in Florence during his lifetime, where in fact they would have burned him at the stake if they could. His fame only spread later, and in this Boccaccio played a part, giving lectures at the Badia church in Florence on the greatness of the city's native poet. So by about the middle of the fourteenth century there may well have been many people happy to come forward, declaring themselves to be Dante's friends, and claiming too, perhaps, that it was a girl in their family who was the original for Beatrice. We do know that Boccaccio's stepmother's mother was a Portinari, so the Portinari family, at least, was happy to accept that Dante's Beatrice was their girl.

There is one further piece of evidence, and that is the will of Folco Portinari in which he makes a bequest to his daughter 'Bice'. Another record tells us that this Bice (never Beatrice) Portinari married someone called Simone di Bardi. And that is as much as anybody knows about the reality of Dante's Beatrice.

But there are more things to ponder. What to make of Dante's daughter Antonia becoming a nun while living in Ravenna with her father and taking the name Beatrice? Clearly she was honouring her father, but what would her mother have made of the choice? Gemma Alighieri, the mother of Dante's four children, was still alive; Dante was forever writing about his Beatrice but never once did he mention the existence of his wife. Would Antonia have taken the name Beatrice had she ever been a real flesh-and-blood rival to her mother? Then again, Boccaccio met Sister Beatrice in Ravenna and whatever she may have said to him, it did not deter Boccaccio from asserting the reality of Beatrice nor that she was Folco Portinari's daughter.

Odd though, that Dante should have used the real name, if that is what he did, of Beatrice Portinari. In the *Vita Nuova* he explains the extreme lengths to which he went to conceal the identity of the woman he adored, going so far as to develop a fraudulent relationship with another woman to whom he addressed love poems. Yet within five years of the death of Bice Portinari, he was broadcasting her identity all over Italy. And then he would continue to do so in his *Inferno*, *Purgatorio* and *Paradiso*. It does seem rather strange. In troubadour poetry the practice was to use a senhal, a fictitious name, to conceal the identity of the lady. Why would Dante not have done the same?

6 VIA DEL CORSO

When all is said and done, there is something immensely appealing about Beatrice as one of the great feminine literary eidolons, a young woman who captured the heart of Italy's greatest poet, who won a place in heaven two seats away from the Virgin Mary, and whose ultimate character was that of Love who makes the entire universe go round – that pretty little girl living round the corner from Dante at number 6 Via del Corso, in a house that stands there to this day.

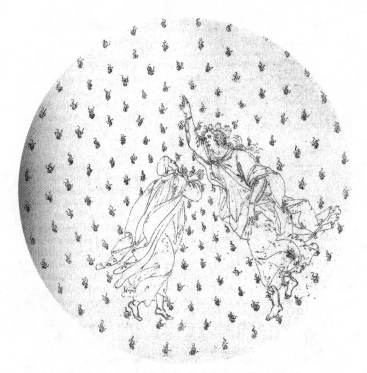

Beatrice guides Dante through Paradise in Botticelli's illustration for the Divine Comedy. *The flames represent divine love.*

DANTE AND THE FAITHFUL FOLLOWERS OF LOVE

After Dante had his dream or vision that Beatrice had eaten his heart (see p.45), he described the experience in a sonnet and sent it to Guido Cavalcanti (c.1255–1300), leader of the Fedeli d'Amore, the Faithful Followers of Love.

The Fedeli were a brotherhood of poets in Florence who pursued an erotic mysticism, first through actual experience with women, then by expressing the experience in poetry. They developed a system for measuring their progress, both erotic and spiritual, as they made the divine ascent through the levels of Love.

While their ladies may have been of flesh and blood, the Fedeli made clear that their ultimate Lady should be interpreted symbolically, perhaps manifested as the divine feminine, Sapienta, the Holy Wisdom.

Influenced by the troubadours, by notions of chivalry and by courtly love, their idea was to regenerate society by achieving a harmony between the two sides of their natures, the sexual and the emotional on the one hand, and the intellectual and mystical on the other. While retaining the notion of nobility in their lives, they would make it depend on personal virtue rather than on inherited wealth or position, and they would achieve spirituality without living a life of withdrawal or celibacy. Their movement looked very much like an attempt to reconcile the conflicting strands in Florentine society – the aristocratic, the mercantile and the religious – which within their lifetimes would tear their city apart.

THE LORD OF LOVE

Dante's sonnet was called *Amor*, or *Love*. He begins by inviting a reply from Cavalcanti and other members of the Fedeli. Then he gives the hour – the first of the nine last hours of the night, the number three or its multiples always being significant for Dante – when the Lord of Love appeared before him in a vision. And then in the final six lines, he says how the Lord held Beatrice in his arms and made her eat Dante's heart, before leaving in tears:

> *He seem'd like one who is full of joy, and had*
> *My heart within his hand, and on his arm*
> *My lady, with a mantle round her, slept;*
> *Whom (having wakened her) anon he made*
> *To eat that heart; she ate, as fearing harm.*
> *Then he went out; and as he went, he wept.*

Guido Cavalcanti replied to Dante, interpreting his dream, saying that Love rules the earth and goes to people as they sleep and takes their hearts. Because Love knew that Death had claimed Beatrice as his prey, Love took Dante's heart to protect her, and though Love wept as he carried Beatrice away, this should be interpreted as joy (dreams meaning the opposite in the morning), because Love knew that Death had been thwarted.

After this Dante was invited to join the Fedeli, which he did. Cavalcanti attracted Dante into the Whites, his branch of the Guelfs, and before long Dante was involved in politics. In 1300, as one of the six ruling priors of Florence, Dante found himself in the necessary but hateful position of having to exile Cavalcanti from the city in order to keep the peace. While in exile Cavalcanti died of malaria. That event weighed on Dante who was still an idealist and not yet convinced from further bitter experience that art was a better means of social transformation than politics. Art can create self-fulfilling prophecies – and that will become the aim of the *Divine Comedy*.

Some have found more to Dante's method than that. They have seen in the poetry of the Fedeli d'Amore a symbolic language understandable only to initiates, and believe that this coded language conveys esoteric meanings. This was true of Dante as well, and Dante himself encouraged the notion. In Canto IX of the *Inferno* he wrote:

> *O you possessed of sturdy intellects,*
> *observe the teaching that is hidden here*
> *beneath the veil of verses so obscure.*

The entire *Divine Comedy*, they have argued, was laden with esoteric meaning and was open to political and heretical interpretations, leading to associations between Dante and the Templars, the Rosicrucians and the Freemasons, all of them transmitters of the secrets.

❊ CHAPTER THREE ❊

The Divine Comedy

D ante is sometimes called a medieval poet, but
although he was writing at a time when England
and France were still in the Middle Ages, late
thirteenth-century Italy was not. Along with his friend the
painter Giotto, Dante is a precursor of the Renaissance, one
of those men who made the Renaissance happen.

Written in his native Tuscan
instead of the more prestigious
Latin, the *Divine Comedy* is no
pious recounting of Christian
truisms; it's an extraordinary
adventure through space and time
that challenges the conventions
and doctrines of the age.

Dante is a fearless writer,
condemning and punishing popes
and kings alike, speaking his
mind on whether non-Christians
really do belong in Hell, and

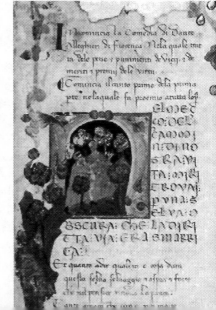

whether others – homosexuals, for example – do too. Though ultimately he keeps within the bounds of orthodoxy, or gives the impression of doing so, his remains a restless and searching mind.

CLIFF-HANGERS AND NARRATIVE DRIVE

Started in Verona in 1308 and completed in Ravenna in 1321, the year Dante died, the *Divine Comedy* is divided into three canticas or books: *Inferno* (Hell), *Purgatorio* (Purgatory) and *Paradiso* (Paradise). Each consists of thirty-three cantos, plus an initial canto, usually considered part of the *Inferno*, bringing the total number of cantos up to a hundred. In the days before the printing press, Dante's *Divine Comedy* would have existed only as handwritten copies, very expensive and for the very few. Instead his epic poem was read aloud to groups of people. That entailed holding their attention by dramatic openings and cliff-hanger endings, and by maintaining a furious narrative drive. Dante did so by inventing the *terza rima*, an interwoven rhyme scheme which is forever tumbling forward. The 14,233 lines of the poem are arranged as tercets, that is groups of three, the first line of the tercet rhyming with the third, and the second line rhyming with the first and third lines of the following tercet – aba, bcb, cdc, ded, efe, and so on – each tercet announcing the one to come.

In the *Divine Comedy*, the Roman poet Virgil guides Dante through Hell, a huge funnel-shaped pit running down to the centre of the Earth. No other living person can enter Hell, and nobody consigned to Hell can ever escape: it is a place of eternal punishment with no remedial element, where the condemned cannot profit from their dreadful experience.

Virgil is the image of Human Wisdom, the best that man can become through his own strength without the grace of God, and so, excellent as he is, he cannot go beyond Purgatory. Instead Beatrice collects Dante in Purgatory, where souls are purged of the seven deadly sins and made fit to ascend into the presence of God in Paradise – which is where Beatrice now leads the poet.

FIRST-PERSON ADVENTURE

Dante's revolution was to write the original first-person fiction. Instantly that turns his epic into an inquiry, and gives it a set of eyes that present us with a live feed from the moment he begins his journey on the night before Good Friday 1300. He ventures first into Hell, then up through Purgatory, and eventually, on the Wednesday after Easter, into Paradise. Dante is a master of images, dramatic and fantastic, yet always remains rooted in human experience. He pities, he admires, he quarrels, he weeps, he embraces; he shares and elicits emotions, even though his characters are dead.

Images and phrases from the *Divine Comedy* pervade our culture. Botticelli, William Blake, John Flaxman and Gustave Doré have all illustrated his epic; it influenced Chaucer, the Romantics and the Pre-Raphaelites; and it continues to work its way through writers from T S Eliot to Seamus Heaney – and to Dan Brown. There is even a *Dante's Inferno* computer game. Above all, there are those familiar terrible words inscribed on the Gate to Hell: 'Abandon all hope, ye who enter here'.

Dante called his work a *Comedy* because, instead of the doom of tragedy, his poem progressed from a dark beginning to hope and salvation. His first biographer and early great supporter, Giovanni Boccaccio, added the word *Divine* because of what he perceived to be the superhuman excellence with which it handled its redeeming purpose.

The inspiration for his *Divine Comedy* began with Beatrice. Dante's epic poem would be his final exaltation and deification of the woman he loved. As he recorded in his *Vita Nuova* – this would have been in about 1294, four years after her death – he suddenly beheld 'a very wonderful vision', presumably the vision of his great work, the complete *Inferno*, *Purgatorio* and *Paradiso*, which decided him to write nothing more about Beatrice until he could do so in a more worthy fashion. 'It is my hope', he wrote, 'that I shall yet write concerning her what hath not before been written of any woman.' For it is she who will lead him out of the errors of this world and into the divine presence.

THE FUN OF HELL

Though T S Eliot once said that the last cantos of the *Paradiso* were as good as poetry gets, Victor Hugo, who wrote *Les Mis* and therefore ought to know, claimed that the *Purgatorio* and the conceptual complexities of the *Paradiso* were beyond human comprehension: 'We no longer recognise ourselves in the angels; the human eye was perhaps not made for so much sun, and when the poem becomes happy, it becomes boring'. The best imagery, the most outlandish, terrifying or grimly amusing encounters, are found in the *Inferno*, the first part of the *Divine Comedy*. Dan Brown is far from being alone when he says that he focused on Hell 'because it is the most fun', or if not exactly fun, certainly irresistibly fascinating, which for an observer, if not a denizen, it is.

The punishments meted out to sinners by Dante in the *Inferno* are known in Italian as contrapasso, that is suffering in a manner that contrasts with or resembles the sin itself. Take for example the astrologers, sorcerers and false prophets who have been consigned to Bolgia Four of the Eighth Circle. They have their heads twisted round facing their rear, so they have to walk backwards because they cannot see ahead of them.

'A writing pair of legs, which protruded upside down from the earth'. Dan Brown might well be describing this image of hell by Botticelli.

Then there is Count Ugolino in the Ninth Circle, who died of hunger after eating his own children and now spends eternity wiping his lips as he eats the brains of his co-conspirator in infamy. Or the delightful image of the pope in the Third Bolgia of the Eighth Circle with his head stuck into a hole, his legs waving in the air, awaiting the arrival of yet two more popes, simoniacs like himself, who will be shoved into his posterior. Or, for that matter, the lovers Francesca and Paolo, forever locked in their lustful embrace in the Second Circle of Hell.

A Numerology of the Divine Comedy

3 books: *Inferno, Purgatorio, Paradiso.*
9 circles of Hell.
9 rings of Mount Purgatory.
9 celestial bodies of Paradise.
33 cantos per book
(+1 canto introduction at the beginning of *Inferno* = 100 cantos)
14,233 lines
Terza rima: lines arranged in groups of 3, the first line rhyming with the third, the second line rhyming with the first and third of the following group of three: aba, bcb, cdc, ded. Each line with 11 syllables: 3 x 11 = 33
3 = Trinity
9 = Beatrice = Divine Love

SYMBOLS AND NUMBERS

In addition to Dante's powerful imagery, there is also his use of symbolism and numerology. Not for nothing do the last words of Dan Brown's *Inferno* read, 'The sky had become a glistening tapestry of stars'. He is following Dante's *Inferno*, which ends with the words, 'and thence we came forth to see again the stars'. Also Dante's *Purgatorio*, whose last words are 'pure and ready to mount to the stars'. And finally the *Paradiso*, which concludes with 'the Love that moves the sun and the other stars'.

For Dante, contemplating the injustice of his exile and refusing to return to Florence on humiliating terms, the stars were a solace. He could still gaze upon the mirrors of the sun and stars, he wrote, and contemplate, under any sky, the sweetest truths. To observe the circulation of the heavens and the regularity of that movement instilled admiration for the works of God. To look up at the stars was the beginning of the journey towards them. It was a step towards leaving the Earth behind and achieving unity with the divine. And that is what Dante does in his *Divine Comedy*; in the *Paradiso* he journeys with his beloved Beatrice far beyond the surface of this world, to the Moon, Jupiter and Saturn and finally to the outermost stars.

FROM THE DARK WOOD TO THE GATE OF HELL

The symbols begin right at the start of Dante's *Inferno*. It is the eve of Good Friday and therefore the season of death and resurrection. But the date is significant in other ways; the year is 1300 and Dante is thirty-five, halfway through his allotted biblical span of life.

In real life, as the 1,300th anniversary of the birth of Christ, 1300 was declared a jubilee year by Pope Boniface VIII, who promised full remission of sins to those who visited the Basilica of St Peter in Rome. Two hundred thousand pilgrims answered his call and lined the papacy's pockets. In the following year Dante was sent as Florentine ambassador to Rome, met Pope Boniface VIII, and witnessed corruption in the Church at first hand; for the sin of simony, Dante will assign Boniface to one of the deepest circles of Hell.

Finding himself in the darkness of the wood of error, Dante realises he has strayed from the true path. Lost and confused, he seeks a way out. He lifts his eyes to the sunrise. The sun symbolises divine illumination; its rays touch the crest of a hill, the Mount of Joy, and he begins to climb. His way is blocked, however, by three beasts symbolising the sins of worldliness – the leopard of lust, the lion of pride and the she-wolf of avarice – and a fearful Dante is driven back into the dark wood.

Dante and Virgil in the dark wood, as depicted by Corot.

As Dante falls into despair, a figure appears, the shade of Virgil, the poet whom Dante most admires. Virgil is the author of the *Aeneid*, the first-century BC Latin epic poem recounting the journey of Aeneas from his escape at the fall of Troy to his founding of Rome. Along the way Aeneas has a dalliance with Queen Dido at Carthage and descends into the underworld, where he receives a vision of his own and Rome's future.

Virgil, who symbolises human reason, tells Dante there is no easy way out of the dark wood; the beasts of worldly sin will destroy him. Instead he must descend into Hell, which represents the recognition of sin, then climb through Purgatory, which symbolises the renunciation of sin. Only then can they arrive at the Mount of Joy and ascend into the light of God. Virgil will lead the way through Hell and Purgatory as far as Earthly Paradise. He cannot take Dante any farther; that is as far as Reason can go. But when Virgil disappears, a worthier spirit than himself will appear and show Dante the way into the divine presence.

There is another reason, however, why Virgil cannot take Dante farther than Purgatory. According to the doctrinal requirements of the Church, Virgil can never enter into the divine light, into the love of God. Although a virtuous pagan, he is condemned to spend eternity in Limbo simply because he was born a bit too soon, before he could respond to the teachings of Jesus Christ. Dante repeatedly questions this, as in these lines that appear in the *Paradiso* (19:70–8).

> *Suppose a man is born on the shore*
> *Of Indus, and is none who there can speak*
> *Of Christ, nor who can read, nor who can write;*
> *And all his inclinations and his actions*
> *Are good, so far as human reason sees,*
> *Without a sin in life or in discourse:*
> *He dies unbaptised and without faith;*
> *Where is this justice that condemns him?*
> *Where is his fault, if he does not believe?*

Quite simply, insists Dante, to condemn a pagan who was not able to become a Christian because there was no Christianity on offer, is wrong and stupid. Nevertheless, Dante will accept what the Church demands.

By the evening of the first day – it is now Good Friday – Dante is tired and daunted by the journey still ahead. He feels himself unworthy of the promised vision of the divine. But now Virgil explains that he was sent by Beatrice, the woman Dante has loved since the age of nine. She has died and dwells in Paradise now, and symbolises divine love. Seeing Dante stumbling in fear and error, Beatrice descended to Virgil's habitation in Limbo and asked him to show Dante the way. 'Love moves me', she tells Virgil. 'Assist him so that I may be consoled.' What is more, Beatrice has been sent with the prayers of the Virgin Mary, who symbolises compassion, and of St Lucia, symbolising divine light, and of Rachel, symbol of the contemplative life. Realising that such heavenly powers are concerned for the welfare of his soul, Dante's spirits rise and he resumes his journey with Virgil in a mood of optimism and joy.

The poets arrive at the Gate of Hell, above which Dante reads these words cut into stone:

> Through me the way is to the city dolent;
> Through me the way is to eternal dole;
> Through me the way among the people lost.
> Justice incited my sublime Creator;
> Created me divine Omnipotence,
> The highest Wisdom and the primal Love.
> Before me there were no created things,
> Only eterne, and I eternal last.
> Abandon all hope ye who enter here.

The famous line is the last. But the centre three lines are critical to an understanding of Dante's apparent view, which is an entirely theologically correct Christian view. They make the point that Hell is not the Devil's domain, but that rather it is created by God. Far from being home to perverse and arbitrary punishments, it reflects divine justice and love. The word justice is important and appears seventy-one times in the *Divine Comedy*; everything in Hell, Purgatory and Paradise is an example of God's justice. The universe is run by that justice; the only deviants are man, who has free will. But of course the punishments meted out in Dante's Hell are Dante's inventions, and the system he imposes is an allegorical one, the torment somehow matching the sin, usually in a highly figurative and imaginative way. Nevertheless, whoever the inventor of the punishments may be, Dante never doubts the good in God's justice, even if he sometimes he feels pity at its effect – though at other times he is indifferent or even cheers the tormenters on.

THE ANTEROOM OF HELL: THE OPPORTUNISTS

As Virgil and Dante pass through the gate they hear the anguished cries of souls in torment. These are the opportunists, those who pursued neither good nor evil but only their own ever-changing interests. They are the pusillanimous, the people of no fixed purpose, displeasing to God and to everyone else. Dante remarks, 'I never would have believed that Death had undone so many'. In this anteroom of Hell they forever chase a fluttering aimless banner and are themselves pursued by hornets and wasps which sting them, causing blood and putrefaction to dribble down their bodies which attracts feasting worms and maggots.

Among the opportunists Dante recognises one in particular. 'I beheld the shade of him / Who made through cowardice the great refusal'. This is Pope Celestine V, who became pope in 1294 but within months resigned the papacy for fear of contaminating his soul with worldly affairs and therefore his prospects for eternal salvation. Urging Celestine on was a priest called Benedetto who promptly filled his shoes as Pope Boniface VIII, Dante's enemy. Celestine had been a saintly man, but Dante condemns him to the anteroom of Hell because his selfish concern for his own spiritual welfare opened the door to great evils in the Church.

Dante and Virgil arrive at the River Acheron, which circles the rim of Hell, before descending deeper, but the monstrous boatman Charon refuses to ferry Dante across because he is not dead. Virgil forces Charon to take them, but Dante passes out in terror and does not awake until he reaches the other side.

THE FIRST CIRCLE OF HELL: THE VIRTUOUS PAGANS

Having crossed the River Acheron, Virgil and Dante stand on the brink of the great abyss. The poets descend into the First Circle, which is Limbo, the dwelling place of those who have not been baptised, including all the virtuous pagans born before the coming of Christ, and virtuous Muslims too (a number of Old Testament Jews, as well as other nameless Jews, were taken to Paradise by Jesus during his harrowing of Hell). They are not punished, but because they have not received salvation through Jesus, they cannot enter into the divine light of God.

Virgil inhabits a more luminous part of Limbo and here he is greeted by the great poets of antiquity, Homer, Horace, Ovid and Lucan, who welcome Dante among their number, making him one of the six. With them he enters a noble castle and within that a green meadow, reminiscent of the Elysian Fields, known in the classical world as the paradise of the dead. Here he sees heroes such as Electra, Hector, Aeneas and Julius

Crossing the Acheron, courtesy of Charon the boatman.

Caesar, also Saladin standing aloof and alone; the philosophers Socrates, Plato, Aristotle, Thales and Heraclitus among others; and men of science and mathematics, including Euclid, Galen, Hippocrates and Avicenna.

Then leaving their fellow poets behind, the six become two as Virgil and Dante venture deeper, to 'where nothing shines'.

THE SECOND CIRCLE OF HELL: LUST

The Second Circle marks the beginning of Hell proper and its torments. As Dante and Virgil make their way round the dark ledge of the circle they are swept by a powerful whirlwind, caught up in which are the souls of those who surrendered reason to their lust. These sinners will never see the light of reason or know God. Among them are Helen of Troy and her abductor Paris, Cleopatra, Dido of Carthage, and Achilles because of his love for Polyxena, daughter of King Priam of Troy, which caused him to desert the Greeks and be murdered – this according to the version known to Dante – by Paris when he went to the temple to be married.

Dante gives a lot of space and sympathy to the story of the adulterous lovers Paolo and Francesca, who were murdered

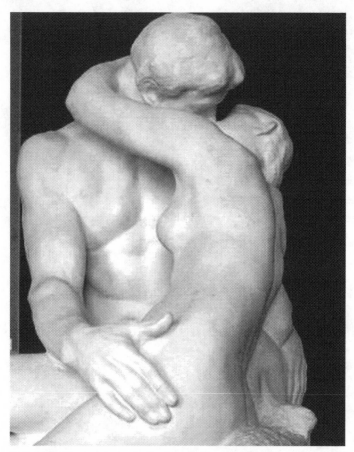

Rodin's The Kiss *took its inspiration from Dante's* Inferno.

by Francesca's husband in about 1286, and are forever locked together naked in Hell. When Francesca is able to pause long enough in the whirlwind to tell Dante something of her story, he is so overcome with pity that he faints. Francesca da Rimini was a contemporary of Dante but her fame, and that of Paolo, greatly increased after featuring in the *Inferno*; the French sculptor Rodin's *The Kiss* was originally called *Francesca da Rimini*.

THE THIRD CIRCLE OF HELL: GLUTTONY

A great storm of putrefaction amounting to stinking snow and freezing rain forever falls on those consigned to the Third Circle. The souls of the gluttonous sinners lie in the slush underfoot where the three-headed dog Cerberus rips them apart with his claws and teeth. The gluttons made nothing of their abilities in their lifetimes, they offered nothing to God; as they wallowed in food and drink, producing nothing but excreta, so now in Hell they themselves are reduced to garbage and filth. Dante's system of punishments in his circles of Hell becomes clear: like for like; as one lived, so one suffers throughout eternity, though usually by grotesque analogy.

The Third Circle serves Dante to introduce prophecy, as happens elsewhere in the *Inferno*. The predictions are highly accurate, certainly in the short term, because although Dante has set his epic in Easter 1300 he really began writing it eight years later, when he had certain knowledge of what had come to pass. In the Third Circle, he is accosted by the shade of Ciacco (the name means 'pig'), a fellow Florentine, of whom he asks what will transpire in 'the divided city', that is his own Florence. Ciacco says there will be bloodshed, set off by 'Envy and Arrogance and Avarice'. In the event, these were the circumstances that turned Dante into an exile from his own city.

THE FOURTH CIRCLE OF HELL: AVARICE

The inhabitants of the Fourth Circle are divided into two raging mobs, each sinner among them dragging a heavy weight. One mob is comprised of moneygrubbers and the other of spendthrifts, and they are forever at war, smashing against the opposing mob with their weights, dragging them apart, then clashing once again.

In life they could think of nothing but money, hoarding it or spending it to excess, and so in these clashes the one excess serves to punish the other. But ultimately their actions are meaningless, as they were in life; the weights are dead weights, burdensome impedimenta. Neither are the shades of the dead recognisable; the features of their souls have been destroyed by their avarice.

THE FIFTH CIRCLE OF HELL: WRATH

It has gone past Good Friday midnight as Virgil and Dante pass from the Fourth into the Fifth Circle of Hell, its boundary marked by a black stream falling over rocks and forming the stinking swamp of Styx. Across the marsh the poets see the countless souls of the wrathful who are forever condemned to attack one another in the slime. Bubbles rising from the ooze indicate the presence down below of the sullen, those who in life refused to acknowledge the light of Divine Illumination and now forever exhale the words of a grotesque hymn.

As the poets are ferried across the marsh of Styx their boat is approached by a swimming soul whom Dante recognises: 'I know thee well, even thus in filth disguised'. His name is Filippo Argenti, about whom we know nothing other than Boccaccio's remark that he was a Florentine of considerable bulk well known for his extreme waywardness and short temper. He was a member of the Adimari family who opposed Dante's recall from exile and confiscated his property, and so here we see Dante settling a personal score. When Argenti tries to haul himself into the boat, Dante shoves him back into the marsh, and then takes delight in watching the other souls in the swamp tear 'the moody Florentine' to pieces before Argenti turns upon himself with his own 'avenging fangs'.

THE SIXTH CIRCLE OF HELL: HERESY

The boat now approaches the flaming towers of Dis, the metropolis of Hell. The towers are described as the minarets of mosques (*meschite* in Italian). Dante says to Virgil 'Master, I can see its mosques clearly glowing red within the ramparts as if they had just been drawn from the fire', and Virgil replies 'Here in inner Hell, the eternal fire that burns inside them makes them red.'

As Virgil remarks, beyond Dis is the abyss with its deepest circles of inner Hell. From there on we encounter the souls of malicious sinners, those who deliberately turned to violence, fraud and betrayal. The mosques of Dis stand as symbols of entrenched evil, of denizens beyond the grace of Christian salvation.

But the poets' entrance to the city is blocked by fallen angels, rebels against God and thus the ultimate in evil. Only when a heavenly messenger strides through Hell and opens the gates before returning whence he came can Dante and Virgil enter Dis. They are now within the Sixth Circle, inhabited by heretics of every stripe, though in particular Dante means those who have denied the immortality of the soul.

Once within the gates the poets discover a vast cemetery with endless ranks of tombs, each with its lid lying to one side, flames issuing from within, forever burning the

The heretics' flaming tombs in Botticelli's illustration.

screaming heretics in their graves. Hearing Dante speaking and recognising him as a Tuscan, one of the damned rises from his tomb. He is Farinata degli Uberti, a leader of the Ghibellines in the wars against the Guelfs during the thirteenth century, who after his defeat was declared a heretic, and who engages Dante in talk about Florentine politics despite realising they are enemies.

They are interrupted by another shade, Cavalcante dei Cavalcanti, known for his atheistic views, and the father of Dante's one-time friend, Guido dei Cavalcanti, leader of the Fedeli d'Amore, whom Dante implies is not the poet he used to be – Dante and Guido found themselves on opposite sides when the ruling Guelfs split into Blacks and Whites (see p.99), but Dante's remark carries their differences well beyond that. When Cavalcanti returns to his fiery tomb, Uberti resumes talking where he left off, as though no interruption, no fires of Hell, can deflect him from his course – and he offers a prophecy, that Dante will be banished from Florence.

THE INNER CIRCLES OF HELL: SINS OF MALICE

As the poets leave the Sixth Circle they stand on a narrow ledge overlooking the inner circles of Hell where the stench rising from down below is so overpowering that they must pause. Virgil takes the opportunity to summarise for Dante the arrangement of the last three circles; first comes violence, then deeper still, because the sin is worse, fraud, and finally at the greatest depth that special kind of fraud that is betrayal. These are the sins of malice and cause the greatest offence to God.

THE SEVENTH CIRCLE OF HELL: VIOLENCE

The Seventh Circle is divided into three rings, each for a different category of violence: violence to others; violence to oneself; and violence against God and nature.

Virgil and Dante make their way down a steep slope of shattered rock caused by an earthquake at the time of the Crucifixion. The slope is guarded by the Minotaur, which menaces them, but Virgil tricks him and they manage to slip by. At the bottom of the cliff is Phlegethon, the River of Blood, which marks the first ring and flows round the circle. Those who have been violent against others are boiling in its stream and any who attempt to emerge more than their punishment allows are shot with arrows by patrolling centaurs. One of the centaurs, called Nessus, carries Virgil and Dante across the shallowest part of the stream and points out to Dante along the way the shades of various conquerors, tyrants, highwaymen and assassins that are being boiled. Immersed in the deepest part of the river are Alexander the Great, up to his eyelashes in blood, and with him Attila the Hun. The Minotaur and the centaurs are symbolically significant; the former is half man, half bull, and the latter are half man, half horse; in each case they are half beast, which says something about those sinners condemned to this circle.

After crossing the River of Blood the poets come to the Wood of the Suicides, whose souls have transformed into withered and poisonous trees whose leaves are eaten by ravenous harpies. Again there is symbolism in the harpies, who have the bodies and claws of birds and the faces of women pale with hunger; they represent the will to self-destruction. Only as their limbs bleed from being picked at by the harpies are the souls in the trees able to speak; they who have destroyed their bodies can speak only as they are being destroyed. Also in this second ring are the souls of the profligates, those who have destroyed their lives by destroying the resources – money and property – by which life is maintained; they are forever chased and mauled by vicious dogs.

Pressing on to the third ring, Dante and Virgil arrive at a great desert of burning sand where a fiery rain falls forever from the sky. Depending on the nature of their offence against God, those condemned here are exposed to a greater or lesser suffering. The blasphemers suffer most of all, for they are stretched supine upon the sand; the sodomites run in endless circles; and the usurers seek what comfort they can by huddling in the desert. The symbolism of the landscape is evident; the desert and the burning heat represent sterility and wrath, just as usury, sodomy and blasphemy are counted as unnatural and sterile actions.

Yet for all that, it is here that Dante encounters Brunetto Latini, his former teacher, for whom he has the highest regard and affection as a man, a writer and a mentor. For one thing, Dante would not condemn Latini's homosexuality.

> 'If my entreaty wholly were fulfilled',
> Replied I to him, 'not yet would you be
> In banishment from human nature placed ...'

And for another, Dante will always honour him for helping him to write, which allows the poet to achieve eternity through his words.

> 'You taught me how a man becomes eternal;
> And how much I am grateful, while I live
> Behoves that in my language be discerned.'

This is one of several examples in the *Divine Comedy* where Dante places someone he values in Hell, but only because he is following the doctrinal requirements of the Church. Virgil is the outstanding case; Brunetto Latini is another. While Dante gives every appearance of accepting Church doctrine, the question remains whether he believed everything he wrote.

THE EIGHTH CIRCLE OF HELL: FRAUD

A steep cliff drops from the Seventh Circle to the Eighth. To make the descent, Virgil arranges that the poets should ride on the back of Geryon, a winged monster of fraud with the face of a just man but with the claws of a beast and the tail of a scorpion. The Eighth Circle of Hell is called Malebolge, which means the Evil Ditches or Pockets; there are ten of these, each called a bolgia. Arranged concentrically, and connected by radial bridges of stone, they become smaller and smaller the deeper they are within the Eighth Circle, each pocket or chasm containing a different sort of fraudster.

Bolgia One contains panderers and seducers, among them Jason of the Argonauts who gained the help of Medea for his voyage by seducing her, only to abandon her later for another woman.

Bolgia Two is inhabited by flatterers.

Bolgia Three contains those guilty of simony, that is the selling of spiritual things, whether positions or sacraments, by the Church. This is effectively what Pope Boniface VIII did in the jubilee year of 1300, when Dante witnessed first-hand the selling of indulgences by the pope. From that moment Dante saw Boniface as corruption incarnate and loathed him possibly more than any man on Earth. As Boniface was not dead at Eastertime 1300, the date that Dante's journey into Hell takes place, he is not included here, but Dante has placed Pope Nicholas III in the third bolgia, along with two of his successors, Boniface and Clement V, whom he denounces for the same offence. Nicholas is already placed head first in a hole in the rock, his feet kicking in the air, his soles aflame; clearly, Boniface will shortly be shoved head first into Nicholas' backside, and Clement shoved into Boniface after that.

Bolgia Four is for sorcerers, astrologers and other sorts of false prophets, their heads twisted round so that they cannot see ahead of them and are forced to walk backwards.

Bolgia Five holds corrupt politicians who are immersed in a lake of boiling pitch, symbolising the dark secrecy of their wheeling and dealing.

Bolgia Six is the confine of hypocrites, who wear gilded lead cloaks and walk about listlessly, born down by the weight of their falsity. Also here is Caiaphas, the high priest of the Temple at Jerusalem who was responsible for having Jesus crucified; his fate is to be crucified to the ground and endlessly trampled upon.

Bolgia Seven is for thieves who are now chased by lizards and snakes that bite at them, and bit by bit steal their very substance and identity.

Bolgia Eight is reserved for fraudulent advisors and evil counsellors. Oddly, Ulysses is in Hell for his deception of the Trojan Horse; he tells the story of his final voyage (a complete invention by Dante) to the end of the earth where his ship founders near Mount Purgatory. This is the spot from which Dante ascends towards Paradise, whereas the unbaptised Ulysses' ship went down, and he drowned.

Bolgia Nine is for the sowers of discord. Just as they divided others in life, so a demon hacks them apart with a sword, waits for their bodies to heal, and then hacks them apart again. Among the condemned are Mohammed, whom Dante regarded not as the founder of a new religion but as a schismatic who created an offshoot of Christianity. Mohammed's son-in-law Ali, who became the fourth caliph, is also among the sowers of discord for his role in contributing to the Sunni-Shia split in Islam.

Bolgia Ten holds alchemists, perjurers, impostors and counterfeiters among its many types of falsifiers. They are afflicted by diseases just as they were a disease on society.

THE NINTH CIRCLE OF HELL: BETRAYAL

As Dante and Virgil leave the Eighth Circle they approach a deep central pit where they see a circle of chained giants as though standing on guard. One of these, Antaeus, the only one unbound, lowers the poets into the depths of the pit that is the Ninth Circle of Hell. The greatest of all sinners, those who have betrayed, are condemned to eternity here, though even they are sorted into four categories and assigned to one of four concentric rounds according to the degree of their depravity.

The traitors do not burn in Hell, however; their heartless and cold-blooded sin means that they are consigned to an equally cold world, the frozen lake of Cocytus, where the graver the sin the deeper they stand encased in the ice. Gravity here is measured in medieval terms, with betrayal of the family counting for less than betrayal of the liege lord. First there is the round for those who have betrayed their families; the second is for those who have betrayed their communities; the third round is reserved for those who have committed the yet greater sin of betraying their guests; and the fourth round is for those who have betrayed their liege lords. At the very centre of all is Satan, condemned for committing the greatest betrayal of all, against God.

Round One is named Caïna, for Cain who killed his brother Abel. Those who have betrayed their kin are immersed here in ice up to their necks, allowing them some movement of their heads, which they bow against the freezing wind or to allow their tears to fall freely without sealing their eyes shut.

Round Two is called Antenora, for Antenor of Troy who according to medieval legend betrayed his city to the Greeks. Those who have betrayed their cities, their countries, their parties, are condemned to a frozen existence here. Among them are Count Ugolino and Archbishop Ruggieri degli Ubaldini, one-time partners in crime, now turned viciously against each other. Having conspired together to gain control of Pisa before the battle of Campaldino against Florence (in which Dante fought in the cavalry), the two eventually fell out. Ruggieri arrested Ugolino and his four children and locked them together in the same cell, abandoned without food or water. All that is known for certain is that Ugolino and his children died, but Dante here – in the best sensationalist tradition – uses a story going round that as each child died, Ugolino ate them one by one. Dante here has produced an inversion of the central Christian mystery, the ceremony of the eucharist in which believers consume the blood and flesh of Christ. But the story has another purpose. Ugolino and Ruggieri are sharing the same hole in the ice, and one is eating the other's brains as Dante comes along. It is Ugolino who has been making a meal of it, and Dante pauses just long enough to allow him to wipe his lips on what is left of the hair on Ruggieri's skull before telling the story of how he ate, or maybe did not, his

Botticelli's three-headed Satan devouring Brutus, Cassius and Judas.

four children before he himself starved to death. As a metaphor for the self-destructive conflict between Blacks and Whites that was tearing Dante's native Florence apart, the story hits powerfully home.

Round Three, Ptolomaea, is probably named after that Ptolemy, son of Abubus, who appears in 1 Maccabees in the Apocrypha, inviting Simon Maccabaeus and his two sons to a banquet and then killing them. Treachery towards guests is severely punished, and the sinners here must lie flat on their backs with only their faces above the surface of the ice so that their tears freeze on their eyes and drive the cold deep within.

Round Four, called Judecca, takes its name from Judas Iscariot, the disciple who betrayed Jesus Christ. The sinners here are punished by being completely in the grip of the ice, body and head, unable to speak or move, and contorted into all sorts of grotesque positions. With no conversation possible, Dante and Virgil quickly pass them by and go to the very centre of Hell.

Satan is fixed in the ice where he flaps his great wings as if to escape, but only creates the freezing wind felt throughout the Ninth Circle which more surely freezes Satan in place. In a parody of the Trinity, Satan has three faces. In each mouth he grips a sinner whom he tears apart: Judas Iscariot at the centre, and Brutus and Cassius, the assassins of Julius Caesar, on either side.

> *O, what a marvel it appeared to me,*
> *When I beheld three faces on his head!*
> *The one in front, and that vermilion was;*
> *Two were the others, that were joined with this*
> *Above the middle part of either shoulder,*
> *And they were joined together at the crest;*
> *And the right-hand one seemed 'twixt white and*
> *yellow;*
> *The left was such to look upon as those*
> *Who come from where the Nile falls valley-ward.*
> *Underneath each came forth two mighty wings,*
> *Such as befitting were so great a bird;*
> *Sails of the sea I never saw so large.*
> *No feathers had they, but as of a bat*
> *Their fashion was; and he was waving them,*
> *So that three winds proceeded forth therefrom.*
> *Thereby Cocytus wholly was congealed.*
> *With six eyes did he weep, and down three chins*
> *Trickled the tear-drops and the bloody drivel.*
> *At every mouth he with his teeth was crunching*
> *A sinner, in the manner of a brake,*
> *So that he three of them tormented thus.*
> *To him in front the biting was as naught*
> *Unto the clawing, for sometimes the spine*
> *Utterly stripped of all the skin remained.*

'That soul up there which has the greatest pain,'
The Master said, 'is Judas Iscariot;
With head inside, he plies his legs without.
Of the two others, who head downward are,
The one who hangs from the black jowl is Brutus;
See how he writhes himself, and speaks no word.
And the other, who so stalwart seems, is Cassius.
But night is reascending, and 'tis time
That we depart, for we have seen the whole.'

From here there is only one way out. The poets must climb up Satan's back, and after a long climb through the body of the Earth they reach Mount Purgatory. Above them the stars of Heaven shine. It is just before dawn on Easter Sunday.

ESOTERIC DANTE

O you possessed of sturdy intellect,
observe the teaching that is hidden here
beneath the veil of verses so obscure

Dante, *Inferno*, Canto IX [Mandelbaum translation, as quoted by Dan Brown, *Inferno*, chapter 63]

As described on p.31, Dante was a member of the group of young Florentine poets called the Fedeli d'Amore, the Faithful Followers of Love. They were dedicated to achieving an erotic spirituality, ascending into Paradise through the adoration of a woman. In some cases they idealised their beloved as Holy Wisdom. The Sufis in their poetry did something of the same, which has led some people to consider a link between the Fedeli d'Amore and the East. Such a link might have been established through the troubadours, through pilgrims returning from the Holy Land, or via the Knights Templar, who had been founded in Jerusalem nearly two hundred years earlier and were also well established throughout Europe, especially in Tuscany and in Florence.

The poetry of the Fedeli d'Amore is also full of symbolism and double entendres. Some scholars believe it contains codes to disguise the true meaning of their words – possibly heretical meanings, to be kept secret from the Inquisition. Again, they say, that could point to a connection with the Templars.

THE TEMPLARS IN FLORENCE

From their inception, the Templars were an international organisation. While their purpose lay in the Holy Land, where their task was to protect pilgrims visiting the holy sites and to defend the Holy Land itself, their support came from all over Europe where they held land, collected tithes and received donations from the pious. They organised markets and fairs, managed their estates and traded in everything from olive oil to timber and wool. In time they built up their own formidable Mediterranean merchant fleet, capable of transporting pilgrims, soldiers and supplies between Spain, France, Italy, Greece and the Holy Land.

Although it is usual to think of the Templars as knights on horseback charging into battle, the thrust of their lances depended in a very real sense on a vast network of support, not just from sergeants and locally recruited soldiery in the East but also from men who worked their estates in Europe and never went to war. Such people manned the Templars' houses – their preceptories – as administrators, agricultural workers and artisans of all kinds. By the 1160s, the Templars had already arranged their European holdings, the properties donated to them by the faithful, great and small, into seven large provinces, which extended from England beyond the

Channel to Montenegro on the eastern coast of the Adriatic. These landholdings were the foundations of their power.

The same network of European estates that funded the Templars in the Holy Land developed naturally into an international financial system. During an age of increasing movement owing to the crusades and the growth of trade and pilgrimages, the Templar network of preceptories in the West developed a system of credit notes whereby money deposited in one preceptory could be withdrawn at another upon production of the note. In this way the Templars became Europe's first international bankers.

DANTE AND THE FEDE SANTA: A TEMPLAR SUPPORT GROUP

Such were the activities that the Templars had developed in Tuscany, which was one of the most economically advanced regions in Western Christendom. Since 1138, when the Templars received their first donation in Tuscany, they had built an impressive network of preceptories, with houses at Lucca, Pisa, Arezzo, Florence and many other places. Tuscany was on the trade routes between East and West, and on the pilgrimage routes to Rome and the Adriatic ports for embarkation to the East. Moreover the region was rich in natural resources, including iron and copper, and Florence in particular was famous and wealthy for its wool trade, for which it required finance. The Templar's Tuscan preceptories, therefore, served to supply the Templars overseas, as hostels for pilgrims heading East, and as financial institutions for one of Europe's most vibrant economic regions. When Dante and his brother engaged in buying and selling property, raising loans and negotiating interest and repayments, one can well imagine them dealing with the Templars.

But, according to claims that were first heard in the seventeenth century, Dante's involvement with the Templars amounted to more than that. The matter was investigated in the nineteenth century by none other than Dante Gabriel Rossetti, poet and painter and founder of the Pre-Raphaelite movement in England. Rossetti came to the conclusion that Dante had been initiated into La Fede Santa, The Sacred Faith, a tertiary order of the Templars open to lay people. Certainly the *Divine Comedy* contains considerable symbolism connected with the Templars and the Temple Mount in Jerusalem which had been their headquarters, and not only the reference in the *Purgatorio*, Canto XX, to Philip IV, king of France, being a second Pontius Pilate who 'ruthless' and 'without law ... bears into the Temple his greedy sails'. Is it simply a coincidence, for example, that in Canto XXXI of the *Paradiso*, Beatrice hands over Dante to St Bernard who will bring him face to face with God? St Bernard of Clairvaux, famous as a mystical contemplative, was also in his day the chief promoter of the Templars, whom he described as 'the instrument of God for the punishment of malefactors and for the defence of the just'.

The Templars were arrested in October 1307 and put on trial for blasphemy, sodomy, heresy and various other heinous crimes. Many were burned alive at the stake, a fate to which Dante himself had been condemned. By the time the Templars met their final end, in 1312, Dante had completed the *Inferno*, which evidence suggests he then revised. He also launched an attack on the French king in his next book, the *Purgatorio*, and made further veiled references elsewhere in the *Divine Comedy*. Outspoken as Dante was usually willing to be, he had to take care. Secrecy and obscurity were necessary, as any defence of the Templars or their ideas could be interpreted as heresy. According to one scholar, William Anderson, author of *Dante the Maker*, 'Many of the most obscure allegorical passages [of the *Comedy*] receive their most coherent explanation when related to the crisis of the Templar order'.

EROTIC PARADISE

Whether or not it was the Templars who brought back from the East ideas of attaining Paradise by a mystical transformation of sexual gratification, Dante did not forget his old allegiance to the Fedeli d'Amore, and its desire to rise towards a spiritual world pervaded by eroticism.

In the *Paradiso*, for example, Canto I, 1–3, he writes 'The glory to Him who moves all things penetrates the universe and shines in one part more and in another less'. The English 'penetrates' is an exact translation of the Italian 'penetra', which introduces the *Paradiso*'s subtle but pervasive erotic language.

A few lines later (Canto I, 21), when he refers to Apollo skinning Marsyas alive, he writes of how he drew Marsyas 'from the scabbard of his limbs', in which Dante's chosen word for scabbard in Italian is 'vagina'. Marsyas, for his crime of challenging Apollo the god of music, is brutally decoupled from a woman.

This eroticism becomes progressively more apparent through the *Paradiso*, and is reminiscent of Ovid's amorous poetry and the *Song of Songs* in the Old Testament, for which, as it happens, St Bernard, Dante's guide at the end of the *Paradiso*, composed an allegorical commentary. For all his references to the Virgin Mary, Dante did not seem to have virgins entirely on his mind, nor, for that matter, Christian orthodoxy.

DANTE'S ADVENTURES INSIDE HIS MOTHER

Much more can be made of this, and has been by Walter Arensberg in his book *The Cryptography of Dante*. Arensberg argues that Beatrice is not, in fact, the girl around the corner but is actually Dante's mother Bella. Given all the motherly references Dante makes to his Beatrice, that's not an

Apollo skinning Marsyas alive – Titian's last work. The Divine Comedy *is full of sexual symbolism.*

unreasonable supposition. Following on from this, the principal argument of Arensberg's book is that Dante's entire journey recorded in *Inferno* is a journey through the body of a woman, a woman who may or may not be his mother.

The dark wood is her pubic hair, the mountain beyond is her mons veneris, the gate of Hell is her vulva, the noble castle is her clitoris, the descent to the Second Circle is her vagina, and the city of Dis is her uterus. What has happened, says Arensberg (who studied English literature at Harvard and perhaps should take over from Langdon in Dan Brown's novels) is that Dante was born but immediately wanted to return to his mother's womb, both as a child and as a copulating man, and has been disturbed along the way by fears of incest. It certainly provides a new angle on the idea of the Sacred Feminine, and makes good reading alongside Dante's own *Inferno*.

PYTHAGORAS AND SACRED NUMEROLOGY

Dante's fascination, even obsession, with the world of numbers has long been recognised by literary critics as well as by mathematicians. In fact the *Divine Comedy* is the primary example of literary numerology in the Middle Ages, and for that matter throughout the whole of Western literature.

Dante mentions Pythagoras eight times in his writings, and a further mention of his followers, the Pythagoreans, brings the total to nine – not in the *Divine Comedy*, but in two prose works, the *Convivio* and *De Monarchia*. Dante refers, for example, to the Pythagorean doctrine that numbers are the origin of all things. He does not mean this drily; for Pythagoras, the mathematical principles that underlay the universe gave it a harmony, literally a music of the spheres, to which Dante turned his ear, listening for the divine song.

Pythagoras was a sixth-century BC Greek philosopher and mathematician whose thought combined the spiritual and the rational, and who placed geometry and music at the heart of the workings of the universe. He came from the Mysteries tradition, specifically the Orphic Mysteries, which had a reputation for drunkenness and orgies as well as the crankiness associated with attempts at abstemiousness and purification. They were looked at askance by the authorities, but attracted writers, poets, playwrights and philosophers and proved to have a lasting influence on Greek thought. 'I am a child of earth and the starry heaven but my race is of heaven alone', the Orphic initiates proclaimed.

Pythagoras sought to explain the world, both spiritual and material, by numbers. He made important observations on the arithmetical proportions that govern musical harmony, and his belief that movements of the heavenly bodies produced concordant notes was later expressed in English as 'the music of the spheres'.

The influence of Pythagoras was felt on succeeding generations of philosophers, among them Plato and Aristotle, who flourished in the fourth century BC. Aristotle quoted him in his *Metaphysics*: 'There is geometry in the humming of the strings. There is music in the spacings of the spheres.' But the influence of Pythagoras was most imprinted on the thoughts of Plato, who shared with him a mystical approach to the soul and its place in the material world, and who accepted from Pythagoras the idea that mathematics and abstract thinking provided a secure basis for philosophical thought and for addressing both science and morals. Dante, in his liberal education, imbibed the thinking of Pythagoras.

Viewing everything through a Pythagorean lens allowed for a universe based on a harmony of numbers and geometrical shapes. The medieval world view of a universe based on hierarchy was replaced by a universe of unity, an interconnected cosmic kingdom consisting of heaven above and Earth below.

Dante notes that Pythagoras saw Unity as Good and Plurality as Evil. Therefore it is important to pay attention when Dante writes in the *Divine Comedy*, 'five and six, if understood, ray forth from unity' [*Paradiso* XV, 56–57]. The union of five and six is eleven, which turns out to be a fundamental number in Dante's *Inferno*. Eleven and multiples of eleven are common in Dante; the *Inferno* has thirty-four cantos, but the first canto serves as a general introduction to the whole, so essentially the *Inferno* has thirty-three cantos; *Purgatorio* and *Paradiso* likewise have thirty-three cantos each. The entire *Divine Comedy* is written in terza rima, the pattern of its rhyme scheme being aba, bcb, cdc, ded, and so on, so that the middle line of the first tercet rhymes with the first and third lines of the following tercet – but the lines are always hendasyllabic, that is eleven syllables long. Therefore each terzine has thirty-three syllables, just as each book of the *Comedy* has thirty-three cantos.

Twice in the *Inferno* Dante provides dimensions for Hell. Once he states that the circumference of the ninth bolgia (ditch) in the Eighth Circle is twenty-two miles, and once that the tenth bolgia in the Eighth Circle is eleven miles. There is nothing accidental about this mention of eleven and its multiple twenty-two; twenty-two forms part of the well-known fraction 22/7 which expresses the Pythagorean value of pi.

The entire shape of Dante's *Inferno*, and also the *Purgatorio* and the *Paradiso*, are circular. Dante was well versed in mathematics and mentions in the last canto of the *Divine Comedy* the problem of 'squaring the circle', a mathematical impossibility that Dante uses to illustrate the ineffable experience of the divine:

> *Like a geometer who sets himself*
> *To square the circle, and is unable to think*
> *Of the formula he needs to solve the problem,*
> *So was I faced with this new vision.*

The numbers three and nine occur throughout Dante's writings, and have special meaning. The *Divine Comedy* has three parts,

Inferno, Purgatorio and *Paradiso*. Beatrice is associated with nine, the square and multiple of three. Three is the Christian Trinity, and Beatrice, in Dante's mind, becomes associated with the Mother of God.

Some argue that Dante's obsessive use of numbers harbours a deep mystery, but quite possibly he is simply aligning his own work with the mathematics all around him, as in the motions of the stars, and trying to make his great epic at one with God's universe.

THE DREAM OF THE MISSING CANTOS

Boccaccio tells the strange story of how the *Divine Comedy* was seemingly left incomplete at Dante's death. When his friends and family searched Dante's papers they found nothing beyond Canto XX of the *Paradiso* which ends with 'blessed lights like winking eyes keeping time together'. Boccaccio writes how Dante's admirers were 'outraged that God had not at least lent him to the world long enough that he might have had opportunity to finish what little remained of his work'. Dante's sons Jacopo and Piero, both poets in their own right, even proposed to complete the *Paradiso* themselves.

But they were checked in this 'foolish presumption' when eight months after his death Dante appeared to Jacopo in a dream, all dressed in white, his face shining with a strange light, and taking him by the hand led him to a hidden recess in the wall above the bed in which during life he had slept, saying, 'Here is what you have looked for for so long'.

When Jacopo awoke, he went to the spot, reached in and found the missing thirteen cantos, mouldy and on the point of decay; he quickly copied them and so the *Divine Comedy* was finally complete and saw the light of day and the night of stars.

✳ CHAPTER FOUR ✳

𝕱lorence and the 𝕭lack 𝕯eath

*The Black Plague thinned the herd and paved the
way for the Renaissance... and Bertrand created
Inferno as a kind of modern-day catalyst for global
renewal – a Transhumanist Black Death.*

Sienna Brooks, *Inferno*, chapter 99

The Black Death arrived in Florence in the spring of 1348. At
first the victims felt a swelling under their armpits and in their
groin. Then they began spitting blood. Three days later they
were dead. By the time the last victim was tossed into a mass
grave, a hundred thousand Florentines had died. 'La bellissima
e famosissima figlia di Roma', was how Dante had described
Florence, 'the beautiful and famous daughter of Rome'. But
Florence was both heaven and hell.

FLORENTINE PRIDE AND DESTINY

Tuscany was the heartland of the ancient Etruscans, the
mysterious people from whom it takes its name. They were
settled at Fiesole, a hill town above present-day Florence, from

The Black Death in Florence.

where they traded along the River Arno and farmed its rich valley. If they also had a settlement beside the river, however, nothing of it is known. The Etruscans had a rich and extensive literature, but except for one book, which remains largely undeciphered, it has been entirely lost. Nor have any physical traces of the Etruscans been found at Florence.

The Florentines themselves were happy to claim descent from the ancient Romans. They liked to believe that the octagonal Baptistery of San Giovanni had originally been a temple to Mars; it's certainly very old, but dates no earlier than the fourth or fifth century AD. Immediately to its east, the original cathedral of the city, Santa Reparata, was built in the sixth or seventh century and named for a third-century Palestinian martyr executed for refusing to sacrifice to the gods. This was the cathedral that Dante knew as a child. In about 1296, however, when Dante was in his early thirties, he would have watched as it was reduced to its foundations to build the vast domed church we see today – Santa Maria del Fiore, Saint Mary of the Flowers, though usually simply called the Duomo, the cathedral.

Founded by Augustus as a military camp, Florence was set amid countryside filled with meadows and flowers. That's one possible explanation for its name – the Italian version, Firenze, derives from its older Latin name Florentia, the place of flowers. The outline of the Roman walls is still evident in the plan of Florence today. They coincide with the modern Via dei Tornabuoni to the west, Via dei Cerritani to the north, then, making a corner at the Piazza del Duomo, they ran along the line of the Via del Proconsolo to the east. To the south the walls stood back from the then-marshy shore of the river and ran along the line of the Borgo Santi Apostoli; an outpost commanded the head of the Ponte Vecchio.

The great space that is the Piazza della Republica at the centre of the city was the Mercato Vecchio, the old medieval market that occupied the forum of Roman times. The crossroads of the ancient city was here, the intersection of the cardo maximus that ran north–south along the line of the present-day Via Roma, and the east–west decumanus maximus along the line of the Via del Corso. Walk east along the Via del Corso, a narrow street today, and you come to the Palazzo Portinari Salviati at number 6, where Beatrice Portinari was born. Dante was born very close by, though the exact location of his house is unknown. Here among the pattern of the ancient Roman streets was the Florence that Dante loved, the city that was Dante's world.

Hardly anything now remains of Florence's Roman past. The shape of the Roman amphitheatre can still be discerned in the curve of the Via Torta and the Via dei Bentaccordi. The oldest standing structure in Florence is Byzantine, the Pagliazzi Tower, which now forms part of the Hotel Brunelleschi, much loved by Robert Langdon, and where he stays while recuperating at the end of his adventures in *Inferno*.

These remains were similarly slight in Dante's day. What counted for the Florentines, however, was the superimposition of their lives on the outline and street plan of the ancient past, a sufficient sensation for Dante and other Florentines to claim themselves as the heirs of Rome – and also to project a sense of greatness into a future that was yet to be born.

FLORENCE REBORN

Situated in the valley of the Arno, the richest farmland in Tuscany, and standing astride the trade and pilgrimage routes between East and West, Florence had become a prosperous mercantile city by Dante's time.

Much of its wealth came from the wool industry, which imported fine English wool, the best in the world. After being washed in the Arno, combed, spun into yarn and woven on wooden looms, the wool was dyed intense and beautiful colours, ranging from the sparkling yellow obtained from crocuses growing in the high Tuscan meadows to brilliant vermilion derived from cinnabar gathered near the Pyramids of Giza. The manufacture and trade in wool required financing, so Florence soon developed a sophisticated banking and financial system that found opportunities in numerous spheres well beyond Florence itself.

This newfound prosperity had come upon Florence very suddenly, almost like a gold rush. The wool industry was introduced to the city by Humiliati monks only in 1239, just twenty-six years before Dante's birth in 1265. Until then, and for several decades thereafter, the Florentines were still a very simple people, as described by Giovanni Villani, the historian of the city, writing during the first half of the fourteenth century.

The citizens of Florence lived soberly and on simple food,
spending little, and their manners were often coarse
and plain. They dressed themselves and their wives in
coarse garments. Many wore skins without linings and
caps on their heads. All wore leather boots on their feet.
Florentine women wore boots without ornament, and
the greatest of them settled for a single tight-fitting gown
of coarse scarlet cloth fastened with a leather belt in the
ancient fashion, and a hooded cloak lined with squirrel,
the hood being worn on their heads. The common women
wore coarse green cloth of Cambrai cut in the same
style, and one hundred lire was a common dowry for
wives, two or three hundred being considered excessive
in those days. Most young women were twenty or more
before they were married. Such were the plain manners
of the Florentines, but they were faithful and true to their
commune and with their simple life and poverty they did
greater and more virtuous things than are done in our time
of increased delicacy and luxury.

One consequence of this rapid accumulation of wealth was
a great building boom during Dante's lifetime. The Badia
Fiorentina, which dated from the tenth century, was rebuilt
between 1282 and 1335, and its bell tower, from which Zobrist
leaps to his death in *Inferno*, was constructed in about 1285.
Across the road from the Badia, the Bargello was built from 1256
to 1327. Work on the basilica and convent of Santa Croce, burial
place of Michelangelo, Galileo and other illustrious makers of the
Renaissance, began in 1294; the Duomo was started two years
later, followed by the Palazzo Vecchio where building began in
1299 and continued in its first phase until 1314.

This boom continued after Dante's death in 1321. Between
1334 and 1357 Dante's friend Giotto, painter and architect, built

the bell tower that rises beside the Duomo. The Orsanmichele, sometime church, market and grain store, was rebuilt between 1337 and 1404. The Ponte Vecchio, swept away by a flood in 1333, was rebuilt in 1345 in the form we see it today.

In other words, within half a century, and before the city was struck by the Black Death in 1348, Florence had put in place many of the landmarks by which we know it today. It had gone from being home to a people dressed in 'coarse garments' to the birthplace of the Renaissance.

A TUMULTUOUS CITY

Yet this familiar Florence, the Florence that we know as a treasure store of art and architecture, a pleasurable indoor and outdoor museum, was for Dante a city of danger, violence and extremes, and it remained so right through the age of Leonardo da Vinci, Michelangelo and Sandro Botticelli.

Politically, northern Italy was different from the rest of Europe. Elsewhere there were emperors and kings, but apart from Naples and the Papal States, self-governing city-states were the rule in Italy. Power was shared in various degrees among their inhabitants, making political life in a city-state like Florence, for example, far more complicated than in the feudal world of oaths and obligations elsewhere in Europe. The rising merchant class was challenging the old aristocracy, and both were vying for control of Florence, all the more bitterly in the light of its ever-growing prosperity. Outside forces also took an interest, both the Holy Roman emperor – based in Germany – and the pope in Rome competing to impose their influence on the north Italian states. And while both the nobility and the merchant class of Florence were jealous of their city's independence, in their rivalry with one another they were happy to align themselves with these outside powers – the nobility generally with the emperor, the merchants usually siding with the pope. The former were known as Ghibellines, the latter as Guelfs, in names that belonged to old legend; any other name, like blues and greens, would have served just as well.

In fact precisely that simplicity of identification by colour tags came into play when the Guelfs finally established their dominance in Florence during Dante's youth. They were even helped by Dante himself, when he rode in the cavalry at the battle of Campaldino in 1289, after the all-powerful Guelfs, no longer having Ghibellines to oppose, divided against themselves into Blacks and Whites. Both factions still sympathised with the pope over the emperor, but the Blacks more so than the Whites – so violently so, in fact, that Dante, who was a White, was condemned to be burned alive at the stake for his politics. He spent the rest of his life, from 1301, in exile from his bellissima city – a city that for some time to come would be beset by sectarian strife, scored by invisible but well-understood demarcation lines, and bloodied and abused by family vendettas, gang and militia fighting, kidnappings, tortures and assassinations, as well as extremes of democratic, despotic and theocratic rule.

EYEWITNESS TO THE BLACK DEATH

In Bertrand's letter to me, he sounded quite proud, saying he considered Inferno to be a very elegant and humane resolution of the problem. ... Compared to the virulence of the Black Death, I admit there is some compassion in this approach. There will be no hospitals overflowing with the sick and dying, no bodies rotting in the streets, and no anguished survivors enduring the death of loved ones.

Sienna Brooks, *Inferno*, chapter 99

Giovanni Boccaccio, the earliest biographer of Dante, was an eyewitness to the Black Death when it struck Florence in 1348. Two years later he began writing the *Decameron*, those hundred diverting and often erotic tales told to one another by seven young women and three young men who retreated to a deserted villa in Fiesole to escape the plague down below. Boccaccio preceded his tales with his own vivid description of what he saw during those terrible months, from March to July, when 'upwards of a hundred thousand human beings lost their lives within the walls of the city of Florence, which before the deadly visitation would not have been supposed to contain so many people!'

Venice lost three-quarters of its population, Pisa seven-tenths, and some cities lost almost all their inhabitants.

John William Waterhouse's Pre-Raphaelite painting of the tale-telling youths of the Decameron.

Estimates varied widely, the lowest for Florence being sixty thousand dead, but whatever the exact number, the devastation it wrought upon the city became proverbial throughout Italy, where it became known as the Plague of Florence.

In Dan Brown's *Inferno*, when Bertrand Zobrist leaves a trail of clues that draw Robert Langdon from Florence to Venice and then to Istanbul, he's tracing in reverse the direction that was taken by the Black Death in 1348. His aim is to place his Inferno depopulation device at the plague's historical hub.

The actual origin of the plague, however, lay much further to the east, in China. It eventually reached the Black Sea in 1347. Constantinople, as Istanbul was in those days, was still capital of the Byzantine Empire, and a major port for trade between East and West.

Whether the plague touched Constantinople first and then travelled north into the Crimea, or vice versa, is not clear, but what is known is that Genoese merchant ships calling in at the Crimean port of Kaffa unwittingly picked up the plague, then sailed through the Bosphorus and to Venice, Sicily and Genoa, quickly infecting the whole of Italy. In March 1348, the plague reached Florence.

Boccaccio understood well enough that the plague had originated in the East, but like others of the age he had no idea of its cause nor how it was transmitted. He speculated whether it was 'disseminated by the influence of the celestial bodies, or sent upon us mortals by God in His just wrath by way of retribution for our iniquities'.

SYMPTOMS AND ESCAPES

Preventative steps were taken, 'cleansing the city from many impurities'; public prayers and processions called on divine intercession, the gates were closed to anyone who was sick, and juniper and sulphur were burned in fireplaces until the scent and smoke were so thick in the streets that birds dropped dead off the rooftops. What no one knew was that their enemies were rats and fleas. And so 'the pestilence began to be horribly apparent by symptoms that showed as if miraculous'.

In men and women alike it first betrayed itself by the emergence of certain tumours in the groin or the armpits, some of which grew as large as a common apple, others as an egg, some more, some less, which the common folk called gavoccioli [swellings]. *From the two said parts of the body this deadly* gavocciolo *soon began to propagate and spread itself in all directions indifferently; after which the form of the malady began to change, black spots or livid making their appearance in many cases on the arm or the thigh or elsewhere, now few and large, now minute and numerous. And as the gavocciolo had been and still was an infallible token of approaching death, such also were these spots on whomsoever they showed themselves... Almost all within three days from the appearance of the said symptoms, sooner or later, died, and in most cases without any fever or other attendant malady.*

Some people reacted by choosing to 'shun and abhor all contact with the sick and all that belonged to them, thinking thereby to make each his own health secure', while 'avoiding every kind of luxury', and only 'eating and drinking very moderately of the most delicate viands and the finest wines'. Others took the opposite direction, maintaining that 'to drink freely, frequent places of public resort, and take their pleasure with song and revel, sparing to satisfy no appetite, and to laugh and mock at no event, was the sovereign remedy for so great an evil'.

Then there were others who:

> *kept a middle course between them, neither laying the same restraint upon their diet as the former, nor allowing themselves the same license in drinking and other dissipations as the latter, but living with a degree of freedom sufficient to satisfy their appetites, and not as recluses. They therefore walked abroad, carrying in their hands flowers or fragrant herbs or divers sorts of spices, which they frequently raised to their noses, deeming it an excellent thing thus to comfort the brain with such perfumes, because the air seemed to be everywhere laden and reeking with the stench emitted by the dead and the dying, and the odours of drugs.*

But the soundest of all, thought Boccaccio, were those who 'deserted their city, their houses, their estates, their kinsfolk, their goods, and went into voluntary exile, or migrated to the country parts' – which was what the ten young people in his *Decameron* did, and survived.

FROM BREAKFAST TO MASS GRAVE

Whatever course one took, the inexorable toll of death had its terrible effect on human behaviour:

> *Tedious were it to recount, how citizen avoided citizen, how among neighbours was scarce found any that showed fellow-feeling for another, how kinsfolk held aloof, and never met, or but rarely; enough that this sore affliction entered so deep into the minds of men and women, that in the horror thereof brother was forsaken by brother, nephew by uncle, brother by sister, and oftentimes husband by wife; nay, what is more, and*

scarcely to be believed, fathers and mothers were found to abandon their own children, untended, unvisited, to their fate, as if they had been strangers.

Many people died daily or at night in the streets, but for those who died at home their deaths often went unnoticed 'until the stench of their putrefying bodies carried the tidings; and what with their corpses and the corpses of others who died on every hand the whole place was a sepulchre'. The graveyards were soon full, and with corpses arriving at the churches hundreds at a time, huge trenches were dug in which the dead were piled up 'as merchandise is stowed in the hold of a ship, tier upon tier, each covered with a little earth, until the trench would hold no more'.

The most shocking thing for Boccaccio was the suddenness with which a person could be overcome, could end up in that ditch within hours of waking fresh upon the day:

How many brave men, how many fair ladies, how many gallant youths, whom any physician, were he Galen, Hippocrates, or Asculapius himself, would have pronounced in the soundest of health, broke fast with their kinsfolk, comrades and friends in the morning, and when evening came, supped with their forefathers in the other world!

FROM THE BLACK DEATH TO THE RENAISSANCE

When Sienna Brooks, repeating the views of Bertrand Zobrist, says 'the Black Plague thinned the herd and paved the way for the Renaissance', the reference is to a view held in some quarters that Europe in the early fourteenth century was 'overpopulated', and that the massive cull by the Black Death was, though shocking, good news socially and economically.

The beaked figure of the plague doctor is a recurrent image in Dan Brown's Inferno.

By that reckoning, the deaths of around a third of the population of Europe and as much as half of Italy's population, had the beneficial effect of creating conditions favourable to stimulating a cultural and intellectual renaissance.

Simply put, the argument is that the death of so many artisans, labourers and peasants gave the survivors a scarcity value that allowed them to drive up their wages so that they had a higher standard of living and greater expectations. 'Every vile craftsman of the city now aspired to reach the priorate and the great offices of the commune', as the Florentine historian Matteo Villani put it right after the plague. But not only workers were affected. Land, money, buildings and furnishings that had belonged to the dead were redistributed among the survivors, whatever their class. The remaining population was richer per capita than it had been before, and therefore had higher disposable incomes that could be spent on cultural pursuits.

Yet there is no evidence whatsoever that Florence, or northern Italy in general, had been suffering from overpopulation or in anyway strapped for cash or retarded from pursuing cultural excellence. Indeed, the opposite is the case, as the building programme in Florence before the Black Death demonstrates. Florence had especially flourished since the introduction of its wool industry in 1239, and was still flourishing right up to the Black Death in 1348.

That said, the plague did affect the economy of Florence in one particularly critical way; it transferred spending from families to the state. As Boccaccio wrote, 'How many families of historic fame, of vast ancestral domains, and wealth proverbial, found now no scion to continue the succession!' The great families, as a basis for economic and political organisation, were shattered by the Black Death. Their functions thereafter were largely taken over by the Florentine state.

The Black Death created a new outlook of communal solidarity as opposed to older narrow concerns with family and lineage. Families could perish, but the state was immortal, and from now on the wealthy invested their money in the state. With the aim of promoting social harmony and stability in business, Florence became a corporate economy. Wealthy Florentines were guaranteed a fixed return on their investments in state-sponsored projects, including buildings and the decorative arts, as part of a broader welfare programme that provided aid to orphans, undowered daughters, the poor, the infirm, the sick and the elderly. For workers and the wealthy alike, the state created a more stable environment, but also the means to direct investment towards learning and the creation of beauty. As Giovanni de Medici, the founder of the banker-despot dynasty that would rule over Florence for much of the Renaissance, told his sons, it was not enough to be rich, one also had a duty to embellish the city.

CHAPTER FIVE

Humanism: the Rediscovery of a Better World

When Robert Langdon and Sienna Brooks travel east from Italy to Istanbul, it's not just the route of the Black Death that they're tracing in reverse. Despite all the horror and devastation caused by the infected rats who came from the East, the learning and ideas that the Byzantine Greeks brought to Florence from Constantinople – as Istanbul was known before it fell to the Turks in 1453 – were of far more importance to mankind.

REFUGEES FROM THE EAST

The transfer of knowledge from East to West had been going on for some time even before the Turkish conquest. Scholars, artists, philosophers and intellectuals from the mortally wounded Byzantine Empire made their way to Italy, bringing the achievements of the ancient Greeks and Romans that had been preserved in Constantinople, but lost with the barbarian invasions in the West. To the extent that medieval thinkers had been interested in antiquity until then, it was to discern a divine plan that vindicated the teachings of the Church.

Now however, and in Florence especially, the realisation grew that the Greeks and Romans had inhabited a superior civilisation, and that they had lived the good life without the aid of divine revelation and supernatural sanctions, and without a faith that set the origin and destiny of man apart from the natural world.

Dante, though seemingly embracing the doctrines of Christian faith, had already begun to assert something of this new outlook. No one before him in the Middle Ages would have declared himself the equal of Homer, Horace, Ovid, Lucan and Virgil, nor obliquely protested their confinement to Limbo.

HUMANISM AND TRANSHUMANISM

The knowledge that came from Constantinople was called humanism. It was the realisation that the proper study for man was man himself, and his place in nature; it was a quest for self-awareness and fulfilment. Humanism was the idea that lay at the heart of the Renaissance.

The irony of the journey made by Langdon and Sienna to Istanbul is that they are drawn there by the actions of a man who declares himself to be a kind of humanist, a Transhumanist as he calls himself, wanting to use advances in knowledge to improve mankind by genetic engineering – to create posthumans. In Dan Brown's *Inferno*, Bertrand Zobrist is one of those Transhumanists who thinks he knows what's good for the world. Without regard for any opinion other than his own, he implements his solution to world 'overpopulation' by launching a modern-day Black Death of sorts, albeit

Giotto's tower and Brunelleschi's dome, the twin treasures of Florence's Duomo.

without the death or pain. It's merely the denial of personal responsibility and human fulfilment – the exact opposite of what humanism means.

BRUNELLESCHI'S JOURNEY OF DISCOVERY

The Florentine journey towards humanism can be illustrated in the life of Filippo Brunelleschi (1377–1446), who's most famous for constructing the great dome that crowns the cathedral of the city, Santa Maria del Fiore, known simply as the Duomo. Until the development of new structural materials in the modern era, Brunelleschi's dome was the largest in the world. It remains the largest masonry dome ever built.

But before he could build his great cathedral dome, Brunelleschi had to undertake a journey of discovery, a journey into the past that would show him the way to the future. A journey that was part of the making of the Renaissance.

Brunelleschi was born and raised in Florence, in the Piazza degli Agli just a short walk west of the half-built Duomo, where construction had been going on since Dante's time. From an early age, the boy was fascinated by the nearby building works, by the hoists and cranes used to raise marble and sandstone blocks to the heights of the basilica, and showed a remarkable talent for solving mechanical problems. His early education was directed towards mathematics, and when he reached the age of fifteen he was apprenticed to a goldsmith. In those days goldsmiths were supreme among artisans, their training and their talents placing them well above the rest.

As an apprentice goldsmith, Brunelleschi learned a variety of skills, technical and artistic, from melting and casting metals to engraving silver, decorating with gold leaf, setting precious stones and inventing new designs. Within a few years, however, his talents were overspilling the bounds of the goldsmith's art, and he extended his activities to the decorative inlay of statues, to creating works in low relief, and then to making clocks. He then added sculpture to his repertoire, guided by his close friend and fellow apprentice goldsmith, the sculptor Donatello, with whom he became inseparable for much of his youth. In 1398, at the age of twenty-one, Brunelleschi completed his apprenticeship and was accepted as a master goldsmith.

THE GATES OF PARADISE

Three years later, Brunelleschi became famous throughout Florence owing to his part in a competition whose purpose was to avert the plague. Every ten years or so, the Black Death would revisit the city, most recently in the summer of 1400 when it killed as many as twelve thousand people – about a fifth of the population. The cause not being understood, people sought what remedies they could in the face of the unknown. Most practically, those with means abandoned their homes for the purer air on the heights of Fiesole, or elsewhere in the surrounding countryside. The majority who could only stay in the city resorted to such preventatives as burning strongly scented herbs and other substances, shattering the air with the blasts of firearms or the violent clanging of church bells, or parading a portrait of the Virgin Mary, supposedly painted by St Luke, through the streets.

The notion that Florence was suffering for its sins prompted the Guild of Cloth Merchants to make an offering to whatever outraged divine forces were at work. In 1401, it decided to commission a set of bronze doors for the north side of the Baptistery, the ancient octagonal church of San Giovanni in whose font every Florentine child was brought to salvation in Christ. The twenty-eight panels on the doors were to be filled with scenes from the life of Jesus. Each candidate for the job, however, was asked to submit a trial panel on the theme of Abraham's sacrifice of Isaac, immediately relevant to plague-fearing Florence with its tale of delivery from imminent death. Seven candidates were selected by the guild, all of them goldsmiths and sculptors, and all of them Tuscans. One was Donatello, another Brunelleschi, a third Lorenzo Ghiberti, all of whom were still in their early twenties.

The Jacob and Esau panel on the Gates of Paradise.

According to Giorgio Vasari, in his *Lives of the Artists*, when their proposals were compared 'all were most beautiful and different from one another', but the best was that of Ghiberti. Not that the judges were prepared to let Brunelleschi walk away; they considered his submission so fine that they asked him to share the commission to work on the bronze doors with Ghiberti. Brunelleschi refused, preferring to be first in his own art than equal or a second in a shared work.

For the next twenty-two years Ghiberti worked on the north doors of the Baptistery. There was no question when he finished but that he should also do the east doors, the ones facing the entrance to the Duomo, which took a further twenty-seven years. When Michelangelo saw the east doors a century later he declared them 'fit to be the Gates of Paradise' – the same 'Gates of Paradise' that appear as a clue in Dan Brown's *Inferno*, and through which Langdon and Sienna Brooks pass to enter the Baptistery to decode the message inside Dante's death mask.

BRUNELLESCHI REDISCOVERS ROME

Of far greater importance to the development of European architecture and art, however, was what became of Brunelleschi during the next decade or so. After losing the competition he vowed never to sculpt anything again, and went off to Rome with Donatello. There his imagination was captured by the Pantheon, a great rotunda that was originally built to honour all the gods during the reign of Augustus in the first century BC, and rebuilt by the Emperor Hadrian in about AD 125. In continuous use since its inception, first as a pagan temple and then from the seventh century as the Roman Catholic church of St Mary and the Martyrs, it was the largest domed structure ever built.

Brunelleschi's interest in the city, and curiosity about the past, was something new for those times. He and Donatello spent so many hours exploring the ancient ruins, and unearthing fallen masonry and broken statues, that they gained a nefarious reputation as treasure hunters or worse – practitioners of geomancy, one of magic's seven forbidden arts – in an age when it was still considered an ill omen to uncover pagan remains. They were rediscovering a civilisation greater than their own, however, and their intellectual appetites were keen.

Brunelleschi schooled himself in classical architecture, measuring the columns, capitals and entablatures of the Doric, Ionic and Corinthian orders, and determining the precise ratios of column height to diameter and the proportions between parts that governed their structural strength and their aesthetic effect. He drew every sort of building – basilicas, aqueducts, baths, colosseums, amphitheatres and temples of every shape, round, square and octagonal – and noted how they were held together by vaults, rings and ties. 'So zealous was his study', wrote Vasari, that 'his intellect became very well able to see Rome, in imagination, as she was when she was not in ruins.'

A NEW VISION

Brunelleschi returned permanently to Florence in 1417, and moved into his family home near the Duomo. By now, he had become renowned for his experiments in linear perspective. If knowledge of perspective existed in the classical world, it had long since vanished from Western art; most likely Brunelleschi developed his grasp of the concept through his carefully measured drawings of ancient remains. Around 1413, during one of his visits to Florence from Rome, he demonstrated the technique of conveying three-dimensional perspective in two-dimensional form. His famous experiment involved a mirror and a painting he made of the Baptistery of San Giovanni from just inside the central portal of the cathedral – the view being of those 'Gates of Paradise' again.

Brunelleschi repeated the experiment by painting the Palazzo Vecchio from the northwest, taking in the Loggia and much of the Piazza della Signoria. By analysing the paintings and demonstrating their geometrical principles, Brunelleschi showed how anyone could render painted objects in three-dimensional perspective. Very quickly the technique was learned, and the concept took hold, spreading throughout Europe. A new visual reality was born.

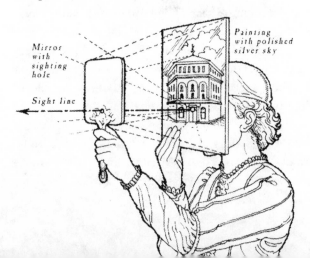

BRUNELLESCHI'S DOME

All this while, however, during the years he spent studying classical architecture in Rome, developing his knowledge of perspective, applying himself to practical building activities, and poring over books and engaging in conversations with learned figures in the city to advance his mathematical and geometrical knowledge, Brunelleschi was preparing himself for the great task for which he had been waiting his whole life. The task he had come to believe that he alone was capable of accomplishing – to crown the unfinished cathedral of Florence that stood near his home.

The foundation stone of the cathedral had been laid in 1296, at just about the time that Dante had been completing his *Vita Nuova*. Now, well over a century later, in 1418, the Guild of Wool Merchants, the richest in the city, who had made themselves responsible for the construction of the cathedral, at last took the decision to start work on the dome. A model of the cathedral bearing a dome, created by an earlier architect, had stood in an aisle of the church since 1367, and a drum to support the dome had been in place for the last five years. No one, however, actually knew how to span such a vast space; to meet these optimistic specifications would require the highest and widest dome ever constructed anywhere in the world.

Everyone understood that the outward thrust of such a dome, unless contained, would cause it, quite literally, to explode. Buttresses like those that supported the great vaults of gothic cathedrals were ruled out as being barbarous German and French inventions, not in harmony with Italian traditions. And then there was the fear that the weight of so vast a dome would cause it to come crashing down. Even if the completed dome could support itself, in the same way that an arch is self-supporting once its keystone is in place, how would it be supported while it was still incomplete? While an unfinished arch can be supported by a frame until the keystone is put in place, there was not enough wood in the whole of Tuscany to construct the massive scaffolding that would be needed to prevent the ever-higher and inwardly inclining structure from collapsing.

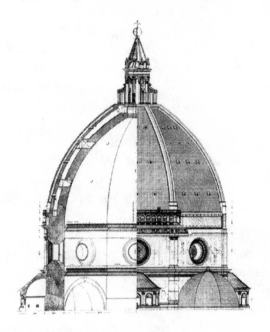

A cross-section of Brunelleschi's dome.

With better luck than he had had in the competition to make the Baptistery doors, Brunelleschi was chosen in 1418 to build the cathedral dome. Quite simply, no one else could do it, and the selection committee of the Guild of Wool Merchants decided that if it could be done at all, they would have to take a chance on Brunelleschi.

Brunelleschi worked on site almost every day until his dome was completed in 1436. He knew the details of masonry construction, and he held his workmen to the most exacting standards; the success of the dome depended on the often extremely complicated geometry of seemingly simple tasks.

To build better and faster, he invented new devices such as multispeed hoists with ratcheting failsafes to prevent falling loads; a hundred years later, Leonardo da Vinci found inspiration in the fertility of Brunelleschi's imagination.

Even modern engineers with the help of computer modelling find it difficult to understand the complex physics that went into Brunelleschi's dome. The man carried a wealth of personal experience and a universe of mathematical and geometrical concepts in his head, and his memory was said to be prodigious.

SUMMER EVENING CONVERSATIONS

Even as he was building the dome, Brunelleschi's mind continued to venture far and wide. Around 1425, when in his late forties, he came to know Paolo dal Pozzo Toscanelli (1397–1482), a brilliant young Florentine mathematician who was then about twenty-eight years old.

In the warm summer evenings, Toscanelli would invite his friends to join him for dinner in his garden. There Brunelleschi would listen to conversations on subjects ranging from astronomy to geometry and philosophy, and himself contribute with his knowledge of Dante, quoting from the poet extensively, remarking on his use of measure and proportion in the *Divine Comedy*, and applying his own architectural instincts to calculate the precise dimensions of Dante's Paradise.

Brunelleschi's fascination with Dante may have had much to do with a shared interest in geometry, and especially the metaphysical symbolism of circles and domes.

THE KNOWLEDGE OF THE GREEKS

Brunelleschi received much of his advanced knowledge in Euclidean geometry courtesy of Toscanelli. Toscanelli in turn felt rewarded by their friendship, which he later called the greatest in his life – a remarkable tribute from a man who knew just about everybody in the cultural and intellectual world of Renaissance Florence. Their shared passions included an interest in Greek geographical and mathematical works, which they tracked down and studied.

When the Greek philosopher Gemistus Plethon was attending the Council of Florence in 1439, Toscanelli made a point of paying especial attention to what he had to say about the travels, cartography and writings of the first century BC/AD Greek geographer Strabo, who until then was unknown in Italy. Toscanelli himself was keen to advance the cause of exploration, and made maps of his own whose accuracy he refined by his readings of the sun and the stars.

THE AGE OF EXPLORATION

It was thanks to Brunelleschi that Toscanelli made his greatest contribution to the age of exploration, which began in the fifteenth century with the great Portuguese voyages down the coast of Africa and out into the Atlantic, reaching the Azores in 1456. A spur to these explorations was the strangulation by the advancing Turks of the overland trade routes that Europeans had long used to reach the Far East. With the fall of Constantinople and the end of the Byzantine Empire in 1453, the overland trade was choked off altogether. Toscanelli had the novel idea that in order to reach the East, Europeans could sail west.

Brunelleschi died in 1446, but by 1436 he had accomplished his great dome. As an old man, in 1475, Toscanelli climbed to the top of his friend's marvellous construction. Inspired by its height and stability, he turned it into a gigantic astronomical device, fixing a bronze plate in the opening at the top so that the sun's rays would pass through an aperture in the plate and fall upon a gauge set into the floor three hundred feet below.

A MAP FOR CHRISTOPHER COLUMBUS

Ostensibly, Toscanelli's giant sundial served an ecclesiastical purpose, in providing a more accurate calculation of Easter and other holy dates. But it served a greater cause than that.

With his more precise measurements of the motion of the sun, Toscanelli was able to draw up extremely accurate tables that enabled sailors venturing into the Atlantic to determine their exact latitude, and thus maintain a course across the trackless sea. Based also on his readings, and on interviews with Portuguese sailors who had gone round Africa to India, Toscanelli drew up a map of the world that placed Asia within reach of a ship sailing westwards across the Atlantic. In 1481, he even sent a letter and his map to an ambitious Genoese sea captain called Christopher Columbus. That was enough to encourage Columbus to take the chance, and thus discover that along the way to China, an entire New World lay in wait.

THE COUNCIL OF FLORENCE

Three years after the consecration ceremony to celebrate the completion of Brunelleschi's dome, the city witnessed an even more resplendent occasion. In the summer of 1439, the leaders of the Greek Orthodox and the Catholic churches met with each other at the Council of Florence, in a desperate effort to unite Christianity, East and West, against renewed aggression by the armies of Islam.

The Byzantine emperor John VIII Paleologus came to Florence in person at the head of a delegation of more than seven hundred Greeks. Both lay and ecclesiastical, they included the patriarch of Constantinople, bishops from throughout Asia Minor and the Balkans, and numbers of learned monks and secular philosophers. The emperor's need was to win Western help to save Constantinople and what remained of his empire from the Ottoman Turks. To do that, however, he first needed to meet with the Catholic delegation of several hundred monks, clerks and prelates, led by the pope. Their immediate task was to negotiate and overcome the various theological differences and conundrums that had grown up between the Eastern and Western churches, and, in the course of hundreds of years, helped to drive them apart.

The sessions of the Council of Florence were held in the church of Santa Maria Novello, and its successful outcome was solemnly announced in the Duomo, beneath Brunelleschi's dome. But ultimately the council proved a failure, because when the Greeks returned home, their concessions were almost entirely repudiated by local churchmen and the Greek laity. To many in Italy and the West, this seemed a wanton act of suicide. There was a streak of fatalism in the East, however, and in their hour of need they felt an especially strong attachment to their old traditions. What's more, they knew that this earthly life is merely a prelude to the everlasting life to come, and they were not about to buy safety in this world at the price of eternal salvation.

GREEKS AND THE FLORENTINE RENAISSANCE

The historical legacy of the council was nonetheless profound, thanks to the presence among the Greek delegation of the Neoplatonist philosopher Gemistus Plethon, and his follower the Greek Orthodox churchman Basilios Bessarion, who gathered together the most complete Greek library in Italy. To these two men an incalculable debt is owed for the progress achieved by humanism in Italy, and so the full flowering of the Renaissance.

The story of Florence as the birthplace of the Renaissance can only be appreciated by understanding how the contributions made by Plethon and Bessarion were born out of their despair as they witnessed the dying days of the Byzantine Empire, and their fear that with its passing they would lose their civilisation, their very world.

THE BYZANTINE EMPIRE

The term 'Byzantine Empire' is a recent invention. It's a label dreamed up by modern historians to describe the eastern half of the Roman Empire – the half that survived the barbarian invasions and extended from northern Italy, through the Balkans and Asia Minor, into the Middle East and along the coast of North Africa. For centuries its capital, Constantinople, was the largest, wealthiest, most cultivated and learned city in the world. For people of that time, however, there was no need to make up a label; they went on calling it the Roman Empire, and people like Bessarion and Plethon called themselves Romans.

The Byzantine equivalent of the barbarian invasions in the West came in 632 with the invasion of the Arabs in the East where the native population – overwhelmingly Christian, otherwise Jewish – were persecuted and oppressed. In response, the Byzantines launched a series of crusades. By 975, their armies had liberated Damascus and most of Syria, and all of northern Palestine to the walls of Jerusalem. But within a century they were confronted by a new and vigorous Muslim enemy, the Turks, who not only reconquered the Middle East but overran all of Asia Minor, and stood on the shores of the Bosphorus opposite Constantinople.

The Byzantine emperor called to the West for help. It arrived in the form of the First Crusade, which recovered Jerusalem in 1099. Successive crusades were despatched as needed; for two hundred years they held back the Muslim advance and protected the Christians of the East. Yet even as Christians in the East formed a united front against the Turks, the Eastern Church in Constantinople and the Western Church in Rome jealously argued the divine inspiration of their increasingly divergent interpretations of Christian practices and beliefs.

THE 'TREACHEROUS DOGE OF VENICE'

Ongoing theological disputes repeatedly led to outright hostilities between the Byzantines and the West. In 1182, a Constantinople mob slaughtered thousands of the city's Venetian merchant population, along with their wives and their children. They were repaid by the so-called Fourth Crusade (excommunicated by the pope), which allowed itself to serve the interests of Greek pretenders to the imperial throne while at the same time being manipulated by Enrico Dandolo, the doge of Venice, to sack Constantinople in 1204.

Despite being nearly ninety and all but blind, Dandolo led the attack in person. He died in Constantinople the following year, and was buried in the south gallery of the Hagia Sophia. This is that same 'treacherous doge of Venice' who's mentioned in chapter 58 of Dan Brown's *Inferno*, in the clue written inside Dante's death mask.

For fifty-six years after these events, the West ruled the rump of the Byzantine Empire as its own prize. It was finally retaken by the Greeks in 1261.

Enrico Dandolo, the 'treacherous Doge of Venice', whose tomb in Istanbul becomes a prime goal in Langdon and Sienna's quest.

BYZANTINE RENAISSANCE

Although for a time Constantinople was again a great emporium, the eastern trade passing through Trebizond on the Black Sea from where it was shipped to the Golden Horn,

Black Sea traffic ultimately declined in the face of further Turkish conquests. Meanwhile, in the absence of a Byzantine merchant marine, the Aegean and Mediterranean trade passed entirely into Italian hands, which gave them a hold over the economic life of Constantinople. Already in 1267 the Genoese had established themselves at Galata, on the opposite shore of the Golden Horn, and even the Venetians were soon back in the city itself.

In 1347 the Black Death struck Constantinople, killing a third of its population. That same year the Serbians seized Adrianople (Edirne), and in 1355 they attempted to take the capital. By then, however, the Ottomans had crossed the Dardenelles into Europe, where in 1363 they took Adrianople and made it the capital of their accelerating empire. Constantinople was threatened on all sides.

Yet throughout this time, and right up to its conquest by the Ottomans in 1453, Constantinople experienced a brilliant renaissance. This revival in learning had started even before the birth of Dante in the West, and amounted to a greater intensification than ever before in the study of ancient Greek literature, philosophy and science, while in art it expressed a new realism in mosaics and painting. The onslaught of the Turks eventually destroyed the Byzantine Empire, but not before the influence of this Greek awakening spread to the West, stimulating and broadening the Italian Renaissance.

CONSTANTINOPLE AVANT GARDE

Something of Constantinople's final story can be read at the church of St Saviour in Chora, standing close by the Land Walls in the western reaches of the city. The church dates originally from the early fifth century, and has been rebuilt and restored several times. Between 1316 and 1321, a new dome was built over the existing nave, the two narthexes and the parecclesion (funerary chapel) were added, and the whole was entirely redecorated. The man responsible for this work was Theodore Metochites, whose mosaic portrait showing him offering his church to Christ can be seen over the door that leads from the inner narthex into the nave. Rising to the position of Grand Logothete, that is chancellor, under the emperor Andronicus II Paleologus, Metochites became a very rich man and a great patron; the decorations in his church have been acclaimed as the supreme achievement of late Byzantine art.

Metochites had known more than power and wealth; he was in the words of one of his pupils 'a living library', and after the recovery of the city in 1261 he refounded its university. A renowned polymath, he was among other things an astronomer, a historian, a poet and a philosopher steeped in ancient Greek learning. The Byzantines had never lost sight of their ancient heritage, and throughout their history could as readily quote from Homer as from the Bible. For some among them, therefore, the route to regeneration lay in their classical heritage, in that unconquerable empire of past glory that lay beyond the military conquests of their enemies. Metochites was a classical scholar, and even as he was presiding over imperial defeats at the hands of the Ottomans in Anatolia, and reflecting in his learned essays on the parlous state of Byzantine society, in the mosaics of his church and most especially in the frescoes of the parecclesion he was eagerly patronising work that broke with the static and two-dimensional iconography of Byzantium.

As throughout Byzantine history, the artists who decorated St Saviour worked anonymously in the service of their patron's wishes. In this instance Metochites was probably actively inspirational, encouraging a return to the canons of the Hellenistic past, so that the figures in the mosaics and the frescoes are placed in a universe of solidity, space and

The Anastasis *of St Saviour at the Chora church in Istanbul.*

movement, allowing dimension for the drama of human thoughts and feelings that play in every face and gesture. To this has been added an intensity of colour and emotion, the drama brought to a peak of urgency and resolve in the *Anastasis* (Greek for Resurrection), the painting in the apse of the parecclesion showing Christ not so much raising the dead as yanking them from their graves. The fresco is conceived and executed with far greater energy than anything attempted by Dante's friend Giotto, who was commencing the movement in that direction in Italy at that time, but remained for the moment some distance behind the avant garde that surrounded Metochites. The *Anastasis* is a tremendous leap into life. It is also a precursor of the European Renaissance.

RESTORING PAGANISM ON THE RUINS OF CHRISTIANITY

A century after the *Anastasis*, at the time when the Byzantine emperor John VIII Paleologus was attending the Council of Florence in 1439, his younger brother Constantine was regent at Constantinople. Four years later, Constantine was placed in charge of the Peloponnese, which he ruled from the mountain eyrie of Mistra, a jewel of Byzantine architecture and art overlooking ancient Sparta. With the Turks ravaging Greece, and amid an atmosphere of grim foreboding, Constantine spent his days with the philosopher Gemistus Plethon, originally from Constantinople and one of the most radical thinkers of the century. Plethon had attended the Council of Florence, which confirmed his belief that Christianity offered no solutions; he proposed the salvation of society through a return to the ideals of ancient Greece, supported by a revived Hellenic religion and an ethical system based on Neoplatonic philosophy. He lectured in Florence on Aristotle and Plato, and was influential in Cosimo de' Medici's founding of the Platonic Academy, where his aim was to restore paganism upon the ruins of Christianity.

When John VIII died childless at Constantinople towards the end of 1448, his brother came from Mistra and succeeded him to the imperial throne as Constantine XI Paleologus. But it was already too late, and by May 1453 almost everything was lost; the Turks had tightly surrounded Constantinople and were moving in for the kill. 'Remember that you are the descendants of the heroes of ancient Greece and Rome', Constantine told his commanders on the eve of Constantinople's fall, 'and be worthy of your ancestors'. Hours later, fighting at the city walls, Constantine was cut down and never seen again. His words, wrote Edward Gibbon, had been 'the funeral oration of the Roman Empire'.

Plethon did not live to see the end. He died at Mistra in 1452. Twelve years later, his Italian admirers removed his remains to Rimini, 'so that the great Teacher may be among free men', and inscribed his tomb with 'Prince of Philosophers of his time'.

The greatest monument raised to Plethon and his fellow emigré Greeks, however, was the spirit of humanism in Florence, which was spreading outwards throughout Europe. The city's fifteenth-century chancellors taught the people that they were the heirs of Rome, and that it was the duty of scholars to immerse themselves in public life. The Medicis, especially Cosimo and Lorenzo the Magnficent, who took their inspiration from Plethon's lectures on classical literature and philosphy, along with those of Bessarion and other Greeks from the time of the Council of Florence, were devoted humanists, enthusiastic book collectors, passionate patrons of the arts, and supporters of Plethon's Platonic Academy. Byzantium may have died, but the writings and teachings of ancient Greek civilisation were kept alive by the scholars and refugees who brought their learning to the West, and instilled the spirit of humanism in Italy.

✴ CHAPTER SIX ✴

Botticelli and Infernal Art

*The masterpiece before him – La Mappa dell'Inferno –
had been painted by one of the true giants of the Italian
Renaissance, Sandro Botticelli. An elaborate blueprint
of the underworld, the* Map of Hell *was one of the most
frightening visions of the afterlife ever created.*

Robert Langdon, *Inferno*, chapter 14

Above all else, we associate Sandro Botticelli with the ethereal beauty of the women in his *Primavera*, and the sensual awakening of his *Birth of Venus*. Each painting is about the nature of love, and has as its central figure the goddess of love.

The name *Primavera* was given to the first painting by Giorgio Vasari, a student of Michelangelo and himself a painter as well as an architect, although he is most famous these days as the first art historian, author of the *Lives of the Artists*. Vasari said the painting 'signifies spring'.

Botticelli's Primavera.

THE STORY OF LOVE

Primavera is rich in meaning and symbolism. At its simplest, it can be described as being like an episode in a fable by Ovid, a story of metamorphosis.

Starting with the three figures on the right, the fleeing nymph Chloris is pursued by the amorous Zephyr; the two become one, uniting in the beauty of Flora. Another scene has yet to unfold to the left, among the three Graces, and beyond them the god Mercury, seemingly indifferent. This much is the initial phase in the metamorphosis of love that is revealing itself in the garden of Venus, who surveys the events from the centre of the painting.

The second painting, *Birth of Venus*, is less visually complicated, but tells a similar story. The newly born Venus, emerging from a seashell, is moved and inspired by the winds of passion; she expresses the dual nature of love, both sensuous and chaste.

Dan Brown's *Inferno*, however, introduces us to another side of Botticelli, when Robert Langdon encounters the artist's vision of the underworld. 'The *Map of Hell* was one of the most frightening visions of the afterlife ever created'. It is grim, dark and terrifying, Langdon says, 'unlike his vibrant and colourful *Primavera* or *Birth of Venus*'. Langdon goes on to explain that 'Botticelli's *Map of Hell* was in fact a tribute to a fourteenth-century work of literature that had become one of history's most celebrated writings ... a notoriously macabre vision of hell that resonated to this day. Dante's *Inferno*.'

Unfortunately, Langdon and Sienna Brooks have to rush off before the professor can tell us more; Sienna's apartment is under siege from a detachment of storm troopers and a woman on a motorcycle with spiky hair, all of whom apparently want to kill them. We're left to find out for ourselves whether it was truly nothing more than a desire to pay tribute to Dante that compelled Botticelli to entirely change the tone and direction of his work, and to descend into the regions of Hell.

RENAISSANCE UNDERCURRENTS

For clues about the currents – and undercurrents – that swept through Renaissance Florence, we can turn to another painting, by Giorgio Vasari (1511–74). Painter, architect and writer on the history of art, and friend and student of Michelangelo, Vasari knew everyone in the intellectual and cultural worlds of Florence at the time.

Commissioned by Luca Martini, a great friend of Michelangelo's and a member of the Platonic Academy at Florence, the painting shows six Tuscan poets and thinkers gathered in conversation. Although they were not all in fact alive at the same time, they were bound together by a common philosophical outlook. All were humanists, men whose concern was the development of the individual human being, and who were devoted to the revival of ancient knowledge and literature.

That did not necessarily mean they were opposed to the Church or to prevailing Christian theology, nor that they stood apart from the conservative social order of the time. They were however acquiring and recovering materials from beyond the confines of medieval Christendom in the West, and not only beyond its geographical boundaries but also reaching into the centuries of Greek and Roman civilisation before the advent of Christianity. Their desire was to explore, create and experiment with new things. There could be tension in their activities. And, at times, they were handling dynamite.

Dante Alighieri sits at the centre of the painting. The Italian Renaissance and the humanist movement could be said to have begun with his epic journey into Hell, guided by the pagan Roman poet Virgil.

Facing Dante is his closest friend, the poet Guido Cavalcanti (c.1255–1300), whose death could be laid at Dante's door. During his brief political career, Dante was instrumental in sending Cavalcanti into exile, during one of the many factional disputes that turned Florence from a shared paradise into a living hell. Guido was the son of Cavalcante dei Cavalcanti, an Epicurean materialist philosopher and probably an atheist, who was denounced by the papacy as a heretic, and whom Dante consigns to the sixth circle of his *Inferno* to suffer eternal torment. Throughout the *Divine Comedy*, as we have seen, Dante gives every appearance of being ruthlessly faithful to Christian theology and its rewards and punishments.

To the left, Francesco Petrarch (1304–74), the poet and scholar who came up with the phrase 'Dark Ages' to describe the period that followed the light of classical antiquity, is attempting to

Vasari's group portrait of six Tuscan humanists. Dante, at the centre, is holding the Divine Comedy.

catch Dante's attention. Both in his person and in his poetry, he was a quieter and more inward-looking man than Dante, whose nature and writings could be violent and extreme. Between Petrarch and Dante, and standing somewhat behind them, is Giovanni Boccaccio (1313–75), friend of Petrarch, author of the often erotic *Decameron*, who idolised Dante and was his first biographer. These four figures wear the laurel crown in recognition of their literary achievements.

PAGANISM AND HERESY

Somewhat further back in the painting, on the left, stand two commentators on the poets' works – Cristoforo Landino (1424–98), a champion of vernacular Italian, and Marsilio Ficino (1433–99). In 1459, Ficino was chosen by the founder of the Medici political dynasty, Cosimo de Medici 'the Elder' (1389–1464), to establish the Platonic Academy in Florence, an attempt to recreate Plato's original Academy in Athens. In this role, Ficino became the first translator of Plato's known works into Latin, and he devoted himself to reviving Neoplatonism. In his philosophical masterpiece, the *Theologia Platonica*, Ficino adapted Pythagoras, the sixth-century BC Greek mathematician, philosopher and mystic, to Christian purposes. Hailing Pythagoras as the originator of the concept of the immortality of the soul, he used his mystical geometry to explain the soul as a circle, without beginning or end, an infinity.

Ficino became mired in controversy when he translated a newly found trove of ancient Graeco-Egyptian hermetic works. These included the *Corpus Hermeticum*, attributed to the man-god Hermes Trismegistos, whom Ficino regarded as a pagan prophet who foresaw the coming of Christianity.

Ficino, who was also a Catholic priest and an astrologer, was directly responsible for making hermeticism a component of Renaissance thought, in which it was associated with alchemy, magic and astrology. His activities ran him foul of the Vatican, however, and in 1489 he only narrowly escaped condemnation for heresy.

VASARI AND THE MEDICIS

As both architect and painter, Vasari was favoured by the Medicis, the illustrious family of financiers and patrons of the arts who followed in the footsteps of Cosimo the Elder and continued to rule Florence through much of the Renaissance. Like many other great Florentine families, they derived their fortunes from the textile trade.

The need to finance their mercantile activities led the Medicis into banking, and soon the Medici Bank extended its services and influence throughout the merchant houses and governments of Europe, to the point that the Medicis themselves became Europe's richest family.

Vasari dedicated his *Lives of the Artists* to Cosimo de Medici I (1519–74), Grand Duke of Florence, who continued his family's patronage of architecture and the arts. He commissioned Vasari to paint the fresco of *The Last Judgement* in Brunelleschi's vast dome surmounting the cathedral of Santa Maria del Fiore, better known simply as the Duomo. He also had Vasari construct the Uffizi, the 'offices' that once housed the city's magistrates and now hold the world-famous art gallery; and commissioned him to finish off his private home, the Palazzo Pitti, across the River Arno.

To enable Cosimo to move quickly and secretly between office and home – and safely too, as assassination in the streets was always a danger – he had Vasari build for him a remarkable aerial passageway from the Palazzo Vecchio, the Florence town hall, via the Uffizi to the Palazzo Pitti. Well over half a mile long, this is the *Corridoio Vasariano*, or the Vasari Corridor, which despite figuring in numerous postcard views of Florence somehow remains largely unnoticed; very few people are even aware of its existence. As Dan Brown has said, some of the greatest secrets are those hidden in plain sight.

The Vasari Corridor crosses the Ponte Vecchio.

SEEK AND YOU WILL FIND

Some secrets, however, are not in sight at all. Take for example
the words uttered by the veiled woman in Robert Langdon's
vision as he awakens in hospital: 'Time grows short. Seek
and find'. This is a four-hundred-year-old Florentine clue, of
which you would only make sense if you make the connection
with Giorgio Vasari. 'Cerca trova', reads the tiny wording
that's effectively hidden from sight forty feet up the wall of
the Salone dei Cinquecento, the Hall of the Five Hundred, an
immense room built within the Palazzo Vecchio at the end
of the fifteenth century to accommodate the meetings of the

Florentine Council. Meaning 'Seek and find', the words are found on a minuscule green banner in the midst of the vast mural of the *Battle of Marciano*, one of six battle scenes that fill the room. All executed either by Vasari, or under his direction, they celebrate Florentine victories over Pisa and Siena.

The enigmatic words were first noticed only in the 1970s, by Maurizio Seracini, a native Florentine expert in high-technology art analysis. He believes they are a deliberate message left by Vasari himself, pointing to the whereabouts of a famous lost fresco by Leonardo da Vinci. It seems extraordinary that Leonardo's massive wall-sized fresco, the *Battle of Anghiari*, could ever be 'lost'; some say the plaster dried too quickly and deteriorated beyond repair, but others argue that it's impossible to imagine that Leonardo did not know the basic techniques of fresco painting.

Seracini thinks Leonardo's fresco still exists; that it's exactly where it has always been; and that when Cosimo de Medici ordered the redecoration of the hall, Vasari simply built a false wall on which he painted his own fresco, leaving Leonardo's intact just inches behind it.

Seracini – who incidentally is the only real, living person to appear in Dan Brown's *The Da Vinci Code*, where he is mentioned for his real-world discovery that Leonardo's *Adoration of the Magi* had been painted over and altered by another artist who totally misrepresented Leonardo's original intentions, and who is also mentioned twice in *Inferno* – has since demonstrated the existence of this hidden wall and of a fresco upon it, the paints of which are the same as those used by Leonardo.

Following outraged protests from conservative quarters in the Italian art bureaucracy, however, the exploratory work was stopped towards the end of 2012. Despite all Seracini's seeking, the matter remains unsolved.

RENAISSANCE MYSTERIES

'Seek and find' leads Langdon and Sienna, via the Vasari Corridor, into the Palazzo Vecchio – that same turreted building glowing in the Florence night skyline that Robert Langdon saw from his hospital window – in which lie deeper secrets still. Cosimo also had Vasari construct and decorate his private study, the Tesoretto, deep within the Palazzo Vecchio, where he could retreat to pursue his interest in alchemy. Vasari later performed a similar service for Cosimo's son, the melancholic and introverted Francesco I, when he built the strangest feature of the Palazzo Vecchio, the secret Studiolo, a windowless chamber decorated under Vasari's direction with scenes laden with alchemical symbolism.

The overall theme of the Studiolo – you can follow in the footsteps of Langdon and Sienna and visit it today – is the magic of nature. It's demonstrated in the celebration of mystical numbers whose symbolism unites the ancient past with the scientific present through alchemy and the manipulation of divine numerology. At the heart of the Renaissance, among men like Vasari, Ficino and the Medicis, sophisticated men of rational learning were at the same time exploring the mysteries of the pagan world.

HUMANISM AND FANATICISM

During the mid-1480s, at a time when Lorenzo de Medici, the Magnificent, was ruling Florence with a firm grip, Botticelli was commissioned to paint his *Primavera* and his *Birth of Venus* by Lorenzo di Pierfrancesco de Medici, the head of a younger branch of the Medici family. Lorenzo di Pierfrancesco, who had been educated by some of the finest minds in Florence, including the humanist Marsilio Ficino, was patron of some of the leading artists of the time, including Botticelli and Michelangelo. Ficino also remained a close friend, and imparted his sophisticated pagan philosophical outlook to Botticelli, working with him to fill his *Primavera* with Neoplatonist and Pythagorean symbolism. In this way the teachings of Gemistus Plethon, the Byzantine scholar whom Ficino had met at the Council of Florence back in 1438, found their way through the generations, to emerge in the sensuous grace and beauty of Botticelli's painting.

By now, a great change was already overcoming Florence. The voice of that change could be heard in the pulpit at San Marco, the Dominican church and monastery in the north of the city. In due course the numbers who gathered to hear that voice grew into so vast a crowd that San Marco became too small, so the voice spoke from the Duomo, the cathedral of Santa Maria del Fiore itself, where it drew such a terrible picture of the damned that his listeners' hair was said to rise with fright. Among those who came to listen was Sandro Botticelli, and the change was working within him too. The voice belonged to a firebrand Dominican friar called Savonarola.

CONTEMPT FOR THE WORLD

Girolamo Savonarola (1452–98) was born in Ferrara, and became a Dominican friar in Bologna in 1475. Clearly troubled by his own desires of the flesh, he wrote a treatise called *On Contempt for the World*, in which he called upon his readers to reject this world of envy, adultery, sodomy and murder. Six years later he was sent as a teacher to the monastery of San Marco in Florence.

There, where it was remarked that his intense green eyes flashed with fire (just as, in Dan Brown's *Inferno*, Zobrist's 'green eyes flashed fire'), he wasted no time in thundering against the Florentines for their sinful ways, their passion for gambling, their perfumes and extravagant clothes, their dissolute carnivals and their sensual pleasures. All of which were destroying their souls and making it impossible for them to enter the Kingdom of God. Prostitutes must be beaten to make them virtuous; he thundered, homosexuals must be burned alive; the books of Plato and Aristotle must be kicked into the gutter; and all those paintings that make the Virgin Mary look like a whore must be destroyed. The Florentines must do what Savonarola would do himself – they must war against sin and live the austere and simple life of the Early Church. And they must replace the present tyranny of Medici rule with a true republic. They must repent.

This was a full-scale reaction not only to Medici rule, but also, whether articulated or not, to everything that the Renaissance and humanism stood for. The voice spoke to the confused, the dispossessed, to all those who wanted power for themselves or power for their God. It took the form of a great popular movement against the rule of the Medicis and in the name of reform. And yet it spoke to Botticelli too, beloved and favoured by the Medicis, a man who knew the humanist circles first hand, an artist who was the Renaissance itself. Something was missing from the mix, and Savonarola seemed to have the answer.

JESUS CHRIST, KING OF FLORENCE

After Lorenzo the Magnificent died in 1492, he was succeeded by his arrogant, lazy and incompetent son Piero. Commonly known as Il Fatuo, Piero was hardly a man able to contend with the two great threats to Medici rule. One came from Savonarola, the other from Charles VIII, the young and ambitious king of France, who renewed old claims on the Kingdom of Naples and had designs on the whole of Italy. Weak and indecisive in the face of these challenges to his rule from within and without, Piero de Medici allowed his authority to slip away. Lorenzo di Pierfrancesco declared his support for the French king, who had pledged to unite Italy and make Florence the new Rome.

By the time Lorenzo di Pierfrancesco entered Florence in the vanguard of Charles VIII's army in November 1494, to the people's welcoming cheers, Piero had made his escape. Throwing in his lot with the revolutionary movement, he dropped the name Medici and called himself Popolano, of the people. He refused any formal role in the governing of the city, preferring to promote cultural activities from the background. No sooner had the French departed, however, than Savonarola preached that:

> *Florence will be more glorious, richer, more powerful than she has ever been. First, glorious in the sight of God as well as of men; and you, O Florence, will be the reformation of all Italy, and from here the renewal will begin and spread everywhere, because this is the navel of Italy. Your counsels will reform all by the light and grace that God will give you. Second, O Florence, you will have innumerable riches, and God will multiply all things for you. Third, you will spread your empire, and thus you will have power temporal and spiritual.*

Flattered by Savonarola, the populace made the friar the effective ruler of Florence. As a cleric and not a Florentine citizen, he was not entitled to assume formal office, but he ruled from the pulpit. His supporters, organising themselves into a political party, ensured that his measures passed through the Council of One Thousand, even as they declared that supreme power was invested in Jesus Christ and hung a great banner across the gate of the Palazzo Vecchio proclaiming 'Jesus Christ is the King of Florence'.

THE BONFIRE OF THE VANITIES

To purify the city and impose his ascetic regime, Savonarola organised armies of children to march about the streets, even going into homes, inspecting and confiscating belongings. Scent bottles, mirrors, fans, necklaces, packs of cards, profane books such as the stories of Boccaccio, musical instruments, portraits of beautiful women, furniture too lavish, sculptures too bare – all such things were seized and burned. The most famous immolation took place in February 1497, when tens of thousands of objects were piled high in the Piazza della Signoria and set alight in what became infamous as the Bonfire of the Vanities.

Among the objects blackening in the flames were paintings considered sensual by the artists themselves, including, it was said, works by Botticelli, who had become a true believer. Many artists, writers and scholars had been deeply impressed by Savonarola's sermons, his sincerity, his vision of a City of God. Michelangelo, who left Florence after the death of Lorenzo the Magnificent and avoided the worst of what was to come, said in his old age that he could still hear the voice of Savonarola in his ears. The poor and middle class were among the preacher's warmest supporters, but he had support among the wealthiest families too. 'There was never such goodness and religion in Florence as in his day', wrote a law student in the city at the time.

BOTTICELLI'S DANTE

In the early 1480s, Botticelli had already started to make a series of drawings for Dante's *Divine Comedy*. Vasari writes that after finishing his work on the Sistine Chapel in Rome in 1482, Botticelli:

Botticelli's Beatrice and Dante in Paradise.

... returned immediately to Florence, where, being a man of inquiring mind, he made a commentary on part of Dante, illustrated the Inferno, and printed it; on which he wasted much of his time, bringing infinite disorder into his life by neglecting his work. He also printed many of the drawings that he had made, but in a bad manner, for the engraving was poorly done. The best of these that is to be seen by his hand is the Triumph of the Faith effected by Fra Girolamo Savonarola of Ferrara, of whose sect he was so ardent a partisan that he was thereby induced to desert his painting, and, having no income to live on, fell into very great distress.

The process that Vasari describes seems to have been a long one. Botticelli is known to have begun the drawings in the early 1480s, for an edition of Dante with commentary by the humanist Cristoforo Landino, successor to Marsilio Ficino at the Platonic Academy, and yet he was still hard at work as late as 1496 or 1497, during the heyday of Savonarola's rule. Neglecting other work, he harmed himself financially, though that must have been due to his own obsessive nature, for just as Lorenzo di Pierfrancesco had commissioned the *Birth of Venus* and the *Primavera*, so too had he commissioned these Dante illustrations.

While Botticelli drew Dante with a growing religious obsession, Lorenzo di Pierfrancesco had his own reasons for backing the project. Dante was a cultural icon for the Guelf factions of Florentines, whose policy at the time was for an alliance with France, but there was also another angle. When Savonarola came to power, paintings like the *Primavera* fell out of favour. Dante, on the other hand, was one of the few authors that Savonarola was prepared to tolerate.

In depicting the torments suffered in Dante's Hell, Botticelli was able both to live up to Savonarola's asceticism, and to explore a host of different ways of representing naked figures. At the same time he carried forward into Purgatory and Paradise the Venus of *Primavera*; as the illustrations show, she is always the same woman.

Like Dante, Botticelli had his Beatrice too. He never married, suffering it seems from an unrequited love for Simonetta Vespucci, the wife of a relative of the Florentine Amerigo Vespucci who explored the coasts of the New World and gave his name to America. When she died in 1476, Botticelli asked that when his time came he be buried at her feet; and so he was, in the Church of Ognissanti in Florence in 1510.

ORDEAL BY FIRE

Slowly, things turned against Savonarola. Poor harvests were leading to hunger, several people died of starvation in the streets, and an outbreak of the plague soon followed. Under the circumstances, the Franciscans, already annoyed by the Dominicans' claim to a special relationship with God, demanded that Savonarola should offer some proof of God's favour.

Meanwhile the pope had placed Florence under an interdict, denying its people the usual rites of the Church. The Signoria, the top government officials elected from the guilds, asked Savonarola not to preach any more. He agreed but said he needed to give one more sermon. When he spoke, he claimed the power of prophecy, the divine right to resist all unlawful authority and the right to attack the Church, which he called a Satanic institution for the promotion of vice and whoredom. This was too much for the Franciscans, one of whom said both he and Savonarola should submit to ordeal by fire. To avoid losing face, Savonarola had to accept, and on 17 April 1498 a great pile of oil-soaked wood was heaped up in the Piazza della Signoria with a pathway running through the middle. There they would pass and by God's grace not be burned alive.

As the rooftops and windows around the square filled with expectant Florentines, the disputants argued over details. Could one take a crucifix into the flames, could the other carry a consecrated host? And then the rain began to fall, a long and heavy rain, and the priors intervened, saying it was too late and too wet for the trail to go ahead.

The crowd reacted furiously, directing their anger and disappointment at the cancellation of the spectacle towards the Dominicans and Savonarola. A huge mob assaulted the monastery of San Marco, and Savonarola was captured and

The execution of Savanarola, as shown in an anonymous painting that's now in the Museo San Marco in Florence.

taken to the Palazzo Vecchio. He was then transferred in chains to the Bargello, where he was tortured and made to confess to heresy. Along with two other friars, Savonarola was condemned to death.

THE EXECUTION OF SAVONAROLA

To ensure that the populace should not be disappointed for a second time, and that every one should have a view as the condemned were led to their execution, a high platform was built from the gate of the Palazzo Vecchio to a gallows that was raised at the centre of the Piazza della Signoria. There, three ropes and three chains hung from a tall post with a transverse beam at the top. The ropes were for the three friars' necks, the chains to hold their dead bodies in the flames when the immense pile of wood surrounding the gallows was set alight.

As the friars were led out from the Palazzo Vecchio early on the morning of 23 May, each was stripped of his robes, leaving him barefoot and dressed only in his undertunic. After his two companions were hanged though still dangling alive, crying 'Jesus, Jesus', Savonarola was led to the vacant place between them and soundlessly dropped. Down below, a man who had been waiting all morning with a lighted torch to set the pile of wood alight called out 'At last I am able to burn him who would have burned me'. Savonarola was hardly dead before the flames closed around his body. In a freakish moment, they burned through one of the cords that pinioned his arms; his right hand rose as if giving a blessing to those who were burning him.

THE MAP OF HELL

Botticelli would have been among that crowd in the Piazza della Signoria. His intention had been to illustrate each canto of Dante's *Divine Comedy*, but by the time of Savonarola's execution he had still not completed his task. He never did. Though Vasari describes Botticelli as producing drawings to illustrate the printing of an edition with commentary by

Landino in the 1480s, the *Mappa dell'Inferno* belongs to a later set, a set that was made during the intense and fiery days of Savonarola's rule. Robert Langdon is wrong when he describes the *Map of Hell* as an oil painting; it is silverpoint and ink, and coloured in tempera on parchment. Neither is it a cross-section; it is a three-dimensional image, a kind of painted sculpture, a new way of representing Dante's Hell that had never been attempted before.

Whatever Botticelli intended when he drew his *Map of Hell*, he had all but completed a journey. With his *Primavera* – playful and bright, and touched with the mystery of Ficino's thoughts, conveyed from the sinless Graeco-Roman world via Gemistus Plethon of Mistra and Constantinople – we feel the early light of the Renaissance. With the rule of the fanatical Savonarola, and Botticelli's descent into Hell, there is a real sense that the Italian Renaissance is coming to an end.

PART TWO

A WORLD IN DANGER?

CHAPTER SEVEN

The Mathematics of Malthus

*Fueled by the unyielding mathematics of Malthus,
we teeter above the first ring of hell.*

Bertrand Zobrist, *Inferno*, chapter 33

D an Brown prefers not to present himself as any sort of activist. He has often said that it's simply part of his technique to put a 'moral, ethical and scientific grey area' into each of his novels, and then 'argue both sides'. It would be hard to read *Inferno*, however, without concluding that he genuinely believes the world to be facing a potentially devastating crisis of overpopulation, and also suspecting that he has at least a certain sympathy with the extreme measures taken by his lanky protagonist, Bertrand Zobrist.

After all, at the end of the book, when the conventions of the genre have been utterly subverted by the success of its villain's scheme to inflict forcible mass sterilisation on the entire human race, *every* character buys into his agenda. They may be somewhat queasy as to whether the end truly justifies the means, but that it's a worthy end is not in dispute. As Elizabeth Sinskey – who, let's not forget, is supposedly the director of the World Health Organization – puts it, 'If we manage to neutralise Bertrand's virus without a viable alternate plan ... we are simply back at square one'.

In interviews to promote the book, Dan Brown told *Time* magazine that 'population explosion on this planet is a very, very serious problem, and could well require some serious solutions'. Speaking to NPR, he went further:

> *Here is somebody* [Zobrist] *who says we have an enormous population problem on this planet and everybody's turning a blind eye, and there are no simple solutions, but there is a solution. And while it's terrifying, maybe there's a silver lining to it. Maybe he's actually the good guy in all this.*

Brown has also acknowledged that he shares the antipathy towards the Catholic church that's expressed by both Elizabeth Sinskey and Robert Langdon when they first meet, in chapter 61 of *Inferno*. In his own words, again to *Time* magazine: 'I am horrified [at] the Catholic church's stance on contraception, and I think it's dangerous'. Catholic commentator Massimo Introvigne responded by charging Brown with promoting what successive popes have called 'The Culture of Death'.

Zobrist's justification for unleashing his genetically engineered virus rests on two highly dubious assertions: that 'by any biological gauge, our species has exceeded our sustainable numbers', and that 'any environmental biologist or statistician will tell you that humankind's best chance of long-term survival occurs with a global population of around four billion.' It's those two statements to which Sienna Brooks is referring when she says 'The mathematics is indisputable', and Elizabeth Sinskey clearly agrees: 'his assessment of the state of the world is accurate'.

Thomas Robert Malthus – known to his students as 'Pop' (as in population).

Apart from the composite graph in chapter 31 of *Inferno*, which comes from *New Scientist* magazine's 2008 report on 'How Our Economy Is Killing The Earth', Brown does not give his sources. It seems reasonable to give him the credit of assuming that he did indeed find scientists who espoused Zobrist's two defining statements. Such views are very far from representing any general consensus, however, let alone from entitling us to see Zobrist as the 'good guy'.

The precise nature of Dan Brown's political opinions is his own business. What else could he mean by the epigraph of his book, however – 'The darkest places in hell are reserved for those who maintain their neutrality in times of moral crisis' – than that he considers overpopulation to pose just such a crisis? He insists that the history and science in *Inferno* and his other novels is 'real'. Given that the 'science' that's presented as being 'mathematically guaranteed' in *Inferno* is used to justify a global-scale eugenics programme, he surely has a moral responsibility to ensure its accuracy.

In this chapter and the next, therefore, we set out to define the 'Malthusian catastrophe' that forms the central theme of *Inferno*. How, why and when did the idea originate, and does the way it's described in *Inferno* reflect the actual state of the world today? Are we really in danger of doomsday?

WHAT DID MALTHUS ACTUALLY SAY?

The power of population is indefinitely greater than the power in the earth to produce subsistence for man.

Thomas Robert Malthus, *Essay on the Principles of Population*

Thomas Robert Malthus was born in Surrey, England, in 1766, took a degree in mathematics at Cambridge, and became a curate shortly before he published the first edition of his *Essay on the Principles of Population* in 1798. Dan Brown quotes its most famous passage in chapter 33 of *Inferno*:

The power of population is so superior to the power of the earth to produce subsistence for man, that premature death must in some shape or other visit the human race. The vices of mankind are active and able ministers of depopulation. They are the precursors in the great army of destruction, and often finish the dreadful work themselves. But should they fail in this war of extermination, sickly seasons, epidemics, pestilence, and plague advance in terrific array, and sweep off their thousands and tens of thousands. Should success be still incomplete, gigantic inevitable famine stalks in the rear, and with one mighty blow levels the population with the food of the world.

Malthus's arguments rest on what he considers to be an incontrovertible mathematical truth, that 'Population, when unchecked, increases in a geometrical ratio. Subsistence increases only in an arithmetical ratio.' To explain that assertion, he argues that while the human population can potentially double every 25 years, it's inconceivable to imagine that food production could increase by any more than some steady, incremental amount year upon year.

Those words 'when unchecked' are important. Although Malthus is often said to have predicted a vast population explosion and subsequent crash, he was in fact describing the 'checks' that kept human numbers from reaching such an apocalyptic level. He believed that the population did indeed fluctuate, but that such fluctuations were swiftly corrected. What's more, while it's the dire warnings of plague and famine that catch the modern eye, Malthus saw the primary checks as being the 'vices of mankind'. As a clergyman he was a little squeamish about spelling out exactly what he meant, but he was basically referring to abortion, infanticide, prostitution and contraception. In other words, what he regarded as the moral failings of humanity served as the first line of defence against overpopulation.

Far from seeking to alleviate the effects of the ongoing cycle of population rise and fall, Malthus regarded it as the natural order of things. He believed that political and philosophical programmes aimed at increasing equality were not only doomed to failure, but morally wrong. As far as he was concerned, 'fatal effects … would result to a society, if every man had a valid claim to an equal share of the produce of the earth', and thus those 'unhappy persons who, in the great lottery of life, have drawn a blank' must inevitably 'suffer from want'.

A visceral disgust for such 'unhappy persons' permeates Malthus's work. When Dan Brown's Bertrand Zobrist describes the mass of humanity as 'cramped and starving, weltering in Sin', he's making an explicit reference to Dante's *Inferno*, but he's also conjuring up a very Malthusian

The Peterloo Massacre of 1819, in which fifteen demonstrators in Manchester were killed during protests triggered in part by food shortages caused by the Malthusian policies of the British government.

vision of overpopulation as the inevitable source of 'vice'. Much like Malthus, Zobrist equates overpopulation with 'sin and hopelessness', and holds it responsible for creating the 'throngs of sickly people' visible in the Doré engraving that he shows to Elizabeth Sinskey. All of which serves to dehumanise the poor to the status of animals, and makes it possible for Zobrist to speak of the Black Death as having 'thinned the human herd'.

Malthus became 'prominent', as Brown puts it, after the publication of his *Essay*. He expanded upon his theories through several subsequent editions, and was appointed to a professorship in History and Political Economy – his students are said to have called him 'Pop' Malthus, short for 'population'. Shortly before he died, in 1834, he was instrumental in the amendment of the Poor Law, which took away the entitlement of unemployed men to financial relief, substituting instead the prospect of the workhouse.

The lasting influence of Malthus's ideas was demonstrated a decade later, when the Great Famine hit Ireland, and the British government continued to export food from Ireland even as its people starved. In quintessentially Malthusian terms, the British official responsible for distributing relief to those affected stated that 'the judgement of God sent the calamity to teach the Irish a lesson, that calamity must not be too much mitigated... The real evil with which we have to contend is not the physical evil of the Famine, but the moral evil of the selfish, perverse and turbulent character of the people'.

Thanks to the perceived ruthlessness with which Malthus and his followers were prepared to allow such population 'checks' to operate, and his overarching disdain for the 'lower classes' as deserving their miserable fate, Karl Marx described his *Essay* as a 'libel against the human race'.

Malthus and Transhumanism

Although *Inferno* depicts the anti-hero Bertrand Zobrist as being equally convinced by both Malthusianism and Transhumanism, there's no intrinsic connection between the two. It's interesting to note, though, how close Malthus came to discussing – and dismissing – some of the central preoccupations of today's Transhumanists.

Malthus devoted much of his original *Essay* towards explicitly countering the upsurge in Utopian sentiments that had followed the French Revolution less than ten years earlier. While professing himself to be 'warmed and delighted' by the recent 'speculations on the perfectibility of man and of society' advanced by French philosopher Nicolas de Condorcet, he considered it his duty to point out the 'unconquerable difficulties' that made them impossible to achieve. As paraphrased by Malthus himself, Condorcet's views now read as a remarkably accurate presaging of the kind of hugely optimistic Transhumanist programmes outlined in Chapter Nine of this book:

> **From the improvement** *of medicine, from the use of more wholesome food and habitations, from a manner of living which will improve the strength of the body by exercise without impairing it by excess, from the destruction of the two great causes of the degradation of man, misery, and too great riches, from the gradual removal of transmissible and contagious disorders by the improvement of physical knowledge, rendered more efficacious by the progress of reason and of social order, he infers that though man will not absolutely become immortal, yet that the duration between his birth and natural death will increase without ceasing, will have no assignable term, and may properly be expressed by the word 'indefinite'.*

For Malthus, such ideas were patently absurd: 'it may be fairly doubted whether there is really the smallest perceptible advance in the natural duration of human life since first we have had any authentic history of man'. Although human life expectancy has

The eighteenth-century French philosopher Nicolas de Condorcet.

in fact doubled since Malthus's day, to be fair that doesn't prove him wrong. He might not have approved of the kind of medical and social programmes that have made that increase possible – especially by hugely reducing infant mortality – but he could argue that they have done nothing to change the 'natural', as in inheritable, human life span.

Malthus did however play a significant role in the development of evolutionary theory. Charles Darwin wrote that he was first inspired to think about the Survival of the Fittest by reading Malthus, and in particular considering how populations would respond to, and recuperate from, Malthusian 'checks'. In Darwin's words, 'I had at last got a theory by which to work'.

WAS MALTHUS WRONG?

It is an acknowledged truth in philosophy that a just theory will always be confirmed by experiment.

Thomas Robert Malthus, *Essay on the Principles of Population*

What's most conspicuously lacking in the original version of Malthus's *Essay* is empirical evidence to support his fundamental premise, of the 'natural inequality of the two powers of population and of production'. Apart from drawing to a certain anecdotal extent on the reported rate of population increase in the frontier regions of the then-new United States, he simply asserts rather than demonstrates.

That makes it very easy to show that Malthus's much-vaunted 'mathematics' were wrong. Malthus explicitly stated that the population could not carry on rising 'even for a single century', and that he had a 'very different view' to that of his contemporary William Godwin, who argued that 'Myriads of centuries of still increasing population may pass away, and the earth be still found sufficient for the subsistence of its inhabitants.' It's now more than two centuries since Malthus wrote the *Essay*, and both population and food production have in fact increased in tandem. It took more than 120 years for the total number of people on Earth to double from the one billion who were alive in 1800. Population growth did indeed accelerate during the rest of the twentieth century, but it has continued to be matched by available food, and the rate of increase is currently slowing down rather than rising exponentially.

To put it simply, both population and food production have expanded at similar rates, and the rate of increase in the food supply has actually been faster than that for population. In eighteenth-century England, for example, a farmer could expect to grow around a tonne of cereal per cultivated hectare; these days, Chinese rice farmers and US maize farmers alike reckon on yields of ten tonnes per hectare.

Insofar as Malthus can be said to have made any concrete predictions, therefore, he got them wrong.

That's a very different issue, however, from saying that the human population can carry on rising indefinitely, without the planet ever reaching maximum capacity. The figure that's cited by the Shade in chapter 22 of *Inferno*, that the global population is expected to exceed nine billion by 2050, is indeed the current estimate from the UN (not the WHO, to whom it's attributed in the novel). That prediction includes a worst-case scenario in which the actual total reaches 10.6 billion.

As is argued in Chapter Eight of this book, the Earth *will* be able to feed nine billion or more within the next half-century. Our resources, and capacity for growth, are not infinite, however, and the population will indeed have to stabilise at some point. What the Shade fails to mention is that the UN report says that that will occur in 2075, when the population will peak at 9.22 billion, and that the numbers will decline thereafter. Exponential growth has in fact already all but ceased in the more prosperous countries of the world, and similar deceleration is confidently expected to occur in developing countries as the economic incentives to have large families diminishes.

Focusing exclusively on Malthus's mathematics in any case serves to obscure the fact that the primary purpose of the *Essay* was ideological. Everything Malthus wrote was coloured by his moral beliefs, and his equations were designed to illustrate his views about equality. Such views continue to be widely held today, and to underpin attitudes and approaches to population issues that can appropriately be called 'Malthusian' or 'neo-Malthusian'.

✳ CHAPTER EIGHT ✳

Apocalypse Now?

For two hundred years, Malthusian fears have receded and resurfaced according to the preoccupations of the time. The last upsurge came in the late 1960s and early 1970s, when world population was growing at its fastest. In their 1967 book *Famine 1975!*, William and Paul Paddock predicted massive food shortages in India within a decade, and advised the USA against giving more food aid because that would only allow more children to be born into starvation.

A year later, in *The Population Bomb*, the American biologist Paul R Ehrlich announced: 'The battle to feed all of humanity is over. In the 1970s hundreds of millions of people will starve to death.' Extreme Malthusians predicted a 'Great Die-Off', in which four billion people would perish by the end of the century,

PAUL McMAHON

FEEDING FRENZY

THE NEW POLITICS OF FOOD

'A superb, highly readable take on food and farming. This is a book we all need to read.' Tony Juniper

This chapter is an adapted version of Paul McMahon's discussion of the prospects for global food production, in his 2013 book, Feeding Frenzy: The New Politics of Food.

Rice being grown on terraced hillsides in Vietnam. Can we feed a world population that is predicted to exceed nine billion in 2050?

while the Club of Rome think tank, in its best-selling 1972 report *Limits to Growth*, used an early form of computer modelling to show that a rapidly growing population was about to run into the brick wall of finite natural resources.

However, Malthusian warnings have always been countered by equally strong ripostes from scientists and economists who have more faith in the human capacity for technological progress and social organisation.

The problem for the Malthusians is that as time passed, their apocalyptic predictions have repeatedly been proved wrong. Thus India in 1975, far from experiencing famine, was despite its rising population self-sufficient in food. Similarly, the new millennium arrived without an ecosystem collapse. The world's population is now seven times greater than when Malthus wrote his treatise. People live longer and are better fed than before.

Nonetheless, we are living through another revival of Malthusian fears. A stream of doom-laden titles have rolled off the presses: Dan Brown's fictional *Inferno* can be added to a list that includes *The End of Food, Famine in the West,* and *Climate Change Peril.* Some of the earlier prophets of disaster insist their predictions are finally coming true. Paul R Ehrlich, now professor of population studies at Stanford, is more pessimistic than ever, telling the *Guardian* there's only one chance in ten of avoiding a collapse of global civilisation. Lester Brown, a champion of population control in the 1970s, writes in *World on the Edge* (2011) that 'if we continue with business as usual, civilisational collapse is no longer a matter of whether but when'. After being almost taboo for two decades, population control is re-emerging as a valid subject for debate.

Neo-Malthusian arguments centre on the idea that we are using up finite resources. Figures are thrown around about how we are running out of land, water, biodiversity, fertiliser or fossil fuel. Climate change is cited as the great new threat, multiplying all the others.

How seriously should we take these warnings? First, we need to assess the biophysical potential for food production. If the laws of biology and physics simply prevent us from growing enough food to satisfy everyone's needs, we have an insuperable problem. For the moment, therefore, let's put economic and political considerations to one side, and pretend the planet is a single system that can be optimally managed to deliver food and other services for humanity. In this fantasy world, how much food can be sustainably produced?

A DOMESDAY BOOK FOR THE TWENTY-FIRST CENTURY

The notion of our planet as being 'crowded' implies that all the good land is already being used. People imagine that not only must any spare land that exists be under forest, but that we are *losing* precious farmland to urbanisation, industrialisation and environmental degradation.

The organisation best placed to know whether that's true, Dan Brown would surely be delighted to discover, can be found in an eighteenth-century palace outside Vienna. The International Institute for Applied Systems Analysis (IIASA) devotes itself to tackling issues like energy and climate change, food and water, poverty and equality. Inside its Habsburg-built headquarters, grand staircases lit by crystal chandeliers lead to rooms with stuccoed ceilings, while outside a former royal deerpark offers a soothing backdrop. However, the mathematicians, scientists, economists and engineers within are more interested in the results coming out of their computers.

Over the past fifteen years, a team led by German mathematician Günther Fischer has pulled together data on soils, terrain and climate – the three factors that determine the suitability of a piece of land for agriculture – to create a map of Global Agro-Ecological Zones. For each of its 2.2 million grid-cells, they have calculated which crops can be grown, and what yields expected, predicting how much food can be

The former Habsburg palace that houses the headquarters of the IIASA.

produced under different farming systems. It's a twenty-first-century version of the Domesday Book, the survey of England commissioned by William the Conqueror in 1086.

The IIASA model shows that about a quarter of the world's land mass (excluding Antarctica) is not productive: 22 per cent is occupied by desert, mountain, inland lakes or rivers, while 3 per cent is used for human settlement. A further 28 per cent is under forest, and 35 per cent covered by grassland or open woodland. Most of our food comes, therefore, from the remaining 11 per cent.

Fischer and his team conclude that 3.1 billion hectares of additional, uncultivated land is agro-ecologically suitable for rainfed crop production. That is, if properly cleared and prepared, this land has the right climate, soils and terrain to deliver acceptable yields, without having to rely on irrigation. If we exclude forest, and protected areas like national parks, the figure drops to 1.3 billion hectares of grassland and open woodland suitable for agricultural expansion – equal to 80 per cent of all the crop fields today.

These figures disguise big disparities. Populous regions like southern Asia, the Middle East and western Europe are already maxed out. North America, by contrast, could expand its cultivated area by more than half, and so too could the Russian Federation and eastern Europe. But the two regions with by far the biggest potential are South America and Africa. Home to almost 60 per cent of the suitable land, they could triple the amount of land under crops.

While IIASA's modern-day Domesday Book does not support a doomsday conclusion, it only tells us what is biophysically possible. In the real world, actually bringing this land into production would pose enormous social, economic and environmental challenges. And there would be trade-offs. The clearing of grasslands and open woodlands would affect the carbon balance, destroy biodiversity and deprive pastoralists of the grazing lands on which they depend.

For that reason, it would be preferable to get more food out of *existing* farmland. There's a huge difference in productivity between the world's most and least developed farming systems. An Iowa corn farmer, or a Vietnamese rice grower, can produce ten times more grain per hectare than a poor farmer in East Africa. Bringing the least productive farmers up to even half the level of the most could double or triple the total amount of food – and help tackle rural poverty in the world's poorest regions.

Can the so-called 'yield gap' be closed? If nature has dealt certain countries a losing hand in terms of soil, terrain and climate, there may be only so much we can do. Thus while northwest Europe is blessed with fertile, humus-rich soils, long periods of summer daylight and the warming influence of the Gulf Stream, parts of Africa are cursed with nutrient-poor soils, variable rainfall, periodic heatwaves and virulent pests and diseases. It's important not to overplay such differences, however. Most populated regions lie between these extremes, and many of those with low-yielding agriculture possess adequate soils and a good climate.

Comparing actual food production with biophysical potential has allowed Fischer's team to demonstrate that no country achieves the maximum attainable yields. Western Europe and eastern Asia get close to 90 per cent; North America only attains 70 per cent; and South America, eastern Europe and Russia produce just under half. But the region that stands out is sub-Saharan Africa, where yields are less than a quarter of what's possible. Large areas of Africa contain fertile soils, abundant rainfall and terrain suitable for agriculture, with maximum attainable yields just as high as in North America or Europe. In theory, African farmers could triple their output without putting any new land under the plough.

The yield gap has more to do with the human environment – poor infrastructure, lack of skills, limited access to finance and technology, unclear land rights, unbalanced trade arrangements and so on – than the natural environment. To quote Akin Adesina of the Alliance for a Green Revolution in Africa, the problems facing African farmers today are 'a result of missed opportunities and decisions made by governments and international institutions rather than a result of stubborn facts'.

So far, we have considered the planet's potential for food production under current conditions. What if the climate changes? Supercomputers the world over are struggling to estimate the potential impact of climate change on agriculture. No one knows what quantity of greenhouse gases will be in the atmosphere; how this will in turn affect surface temperatures, precipitation and plant performance; and the effects of droughts and floods. However, the broad conclusions for the next forty or so years are not as bleak as might be expected. Yes, agricultural production in the mid-latitudes and tropics is likely to be negatively affected, but the high latitudes – places like northern Europe, Canada and parts of Russia – will experience increased productivity. The 2007 assessment of the Intergovernmental Panel on Climate Change actually concluded that global productivity would slightly increase.

That said, the planet is only expected to warm by about one degree before 2050. Things will really heat up after that, which will cause a lot more problems for agriculture. Indeed, the latest research indicates the world is warming more quickly than expected. Thus, while climate change should not prevent us from producing enough food between now and 2050, it's definitely something to be worried about. Feeding a world of nine billion in 2100 might be a much more difficult matter, if we continue on our current path.

TO FINITY AND BEYOND

....

While 'modern' agricultural methods can improve the potential of soils, terrain and climate, there are question marks over their sustainability. The two principal charges levelled against agriculture are that it uses non-renewable resources such as oil, natural gas, and water, and that it destroys our environment by polluting water, shrinking biodiversity, clearing forests and pumping out greenhouse gases.

Concerns about fossil fuels usually run along these lines: in industrialised nations it takes the equivalent of seven calories of energy to deliver one calorie of food; most of this energy is derived from fossil fuels, which will eventually run out; therefore, our current food systems are in danger of collapse. Thus Dale Allen Pfeiffer, in *Eating Fossil Fuels*, argues that in order to return to relying solely on the energy provided by the sun, the world's population will have to fall to a sustainable capacity of about two billion. In ultra-Malthusian fashion, Pfeiffer predicts a great human 'die-off'.

No one expects crude oil to run out within the next fifty years, but it is indeed likely to become scarcer and more expensive. Four-fifths of the energy consumed in food systems in North America or Europe is used to transport, store, process, retail and cook food. There's enormous scope for energy efficiency all along this chain. While diets in wealthy countries might have to become less resplendent, more local, people wouldn't starve; indeed, they would probably be healthier.

The single greatest energy input in modern farming is nitrogen fertiliser; almost half the people on Earth are fed thanks to manufactured nitrogen fertiliser. While there's no shortage of nitrogen in the air, it needs to be 'fixed' via the Haber-Bosch process, which mostly uses natural gas. Many 'doomsters' see this as the weak link in the global food system.

That view was particularly prevalent in the US in the early 2000s, when experts predicted that domestic gas reserves would be gone within decades. Since then, however, the widespread use of hydraulic fracturing (or 'fracking') has turned scarcity to abundance. Although environmental concerns remain about this technology, US natural gas production is up fourteen-fold since 2000. What's more, even if natural gas reserves were to be exhausted, the Haber-Bosch process is not the only way to produce nitrogen fertiliser, just the cheapest. We could turn to other technologies, and power them with renewable energy.

The other critical fertiliser, phosphate, is derived from mining, and thus a more finite resource. Estimates of remaining reserves depend on balancing the cost of extraction against the market price, and vary from the US Geological Survey figure of one hundred years' worth, to a more recent study that suggests more like four hundred years. In addition, most phosphate is eventually flushed into the sea, and there may be opportunities to increase its capture and recycling.

The most important 'input' for agriculture, however, is water. Over the past decade, the notion of 'Peak Water' has become a popular apocalyptic theme. Water is depicted as another finite resource through which we are remorselessly working our way, with agriculture, because it accounts for more than two-thirds of freshwater use, seen as the chief culprit. The same statistics appear again and again: that it takes 1,300 litres to make a loaf of bread; 3,400 litres to grow a kilo of rice; 3,900 litres to rear a kilo of chicken; and anywhere between 15,000 and 100,000 litres to produce a kilo of beef.

But this is a simplification. Most of the water 'used' in agriculture is taken up by the roots of plants, transpired via their leaves as water vapour, and falls somewhere else as rain. The same goes for animals grazing on pastures; most of the water in the grass they eat returns in the form of urine and dung.

Although regions such as northern China, India's Indo-Gangetic plain, and much of the western US are in water deficit, there's no global scarcity of freshwater. Europe only withdraws six per cent of its renewable resources, and Asia only twenty per cent. The problem is not a lack of water, but that water is inaccessible because the right infrastructure is not in place. What's more, farmers use water inefficiently. Almost nine-tenths goes on flood irrigation, which maximises the losses; eleven per cent goes through sprinklers; and only one per cent through drip irrigation, the most efficient by far.

Agriculture is also a major *cause* of climate change. Farming activities are responsible for around thirteen per cent of greenhouse gas emissions. The production and application of nitrogen fertilisers can lead to the release of nitrous oxide, a greenhouse gas three hundred times more potent than carbon dioxide, while livestock production can produce large amounts of methane. Indirectly, agriculture can also be blamed for a large proportion of deforestation. Altogether the production of food could account for close to one-third of man-made annual emissions, more than all the world's factories, cars and planes. To limit global warming, we will have to reduce these emissions.

Legitimate questions surround the sustainability of modern agriculture. We need to find food systems that damage the environment less, while using non-renewable resources more efficiently. The good news is that alternatives exist. Many agricultural systems produce fewer greenhouse gases, or even act as carbon sinks, build soil fertility and preserve watersheds. They also tend to consume less energy. At the same time, they produce large amounts of food at an affordable price and deliver good profits to the farmer. These systems do not require new technology or major scientific breakthroughs, and are being successfully implemented all around the world right now. The challenge will be to scale them up.

FUNGIBLE DEMAND

So far, we have only looked at the supply side of the food equation. What about demand? The Food and Agricultural Organization of the UN (FAO) estimates that the total supply of food will need to increase by seventy per cent by 2050. Food production in developing countries will need to double, and an additional billion tonnes of cereals and 200 million tonnes of meat will be required every year.

These sound like big numbers, the kind that place an enormous strain on agricultural systems. This extra demand is one of the major props in the Malthusian argument, but it's important to place it in context. Demand for food is expected to grow at a slower rate than in the 1960s and 1970s, as the rate of population growth is slowing.

When we remember that global food production tripled between 1950 and 2000, an increase of seventy per cent in forty years does not sound impossible. Moreover, at a biophysical and nutritional level, it is a mistake to regard this extra demand as something fixed, which the food system must deliver at all costs.

An estimated thirty per cent of all food grown worldwide is lost or wasted. In poor countries, that largely occurs during post-harvest storage, or en route to the consumer; in richer ones, much ends up in the rubbish bin. Halving the amount of food waste – a perfectly achievable target – would both reduce the pressure on food supplies and save money.

We can also change how we use crops. If the one-third of cereal production that currently goes to feed animals was consumed directly by humans, it would satisfy the calorie needs of 3.5 billion people. People would not have to give up meat and dairy entirely, just to limit their consumption to animals raised on pasture or recycled food wastes.

The Malthusian doomsday scenario does not stand up to scrutiny. All the science indicates that, so long as we use resources wisely, we have not reached the biophysical carrying capacity of the Earth. Practically every research organisation that has examined this question – from the FAO, to IIASA, to the Office of the Chief Scientist of the UK Government, to university departments all over the world – has concluded that it will be possible to feed the world's population in 2050.

We grow enough food *today* to feed 9.3 billion people. That's what makes it so shocking that the global food system is failing to nourish the seven billion that currently exist, 870 million of whom go hungry because they lack the purchasing power to lay claim to the food they need. Our pattern of food use is a function of political choices and economic disparities, and the ability to change it lies within human hands.

CHAPTER NINE

Transhumanists –
The Eternal Optimists

*I believe Transhumanism is mankind's
only hope for long-term survival*

Bertrand Zobrist, *Inferno*, chapter 66

For many readers, Dan Brown's *Inferno* will provide their first introduction to the concept of Transhumanism. As ever, Brown's fiction is rooted to some extent in truth – so yes, Transhumanists do exist. But who are they, and what do they believe? And, judging from his words and his actions, is the villainous Bertrand Zobrist a typical Transhumanist?

Rather than a single fixed ideology, Transhumanism is a broad philosophical movement that's essentially characterised by an optimistic view of how ongoing scientific developments will affect the future of humanity.

Transhumanists believe that thanks to continuing advances in technology, we will be able to improve not only our physical wellbeing and our lives in society, but also our actual human bodies. What's more, permanent changes will take place at the genetic level, and thus become inheritable from generation to generation. As a result, humans will become a truly different species – posthumans.

ARE WE NEARLY THERE YET?

In a paradoxical sense, our capacity to transcend our physical limitations has always been part of what makes us human. From the moment we first used tools, or wrapped ourselves in animal skins to survive in harsher climates, we began to redefine ourselves as a species. Enough time has passed since the establishment of the earliest human societies that evolution has been able to respond by changing our bodies. Thus, for example, what was once a rare mutation – the continued ability in adulthood to digest milk – proved enough

Printing out the entire human genome for the first time required more than a hundred volumes, each of which held a thousand pages.

of an advantage after the domestication of cows, goats and sheep in the ancient near East and Europe that it became the local genetic norm.

Despite the changes that have already occurred, for Transhumanists it's a matter of definition that we're not yet posthuman. That we will become so, however, is so inevitable that there's little point wasting time in ethical debate as to whether it should happen. Instead, they believe, we should simply embrace the possibilities and focus on what precise form the future will take.

So how will we know when we have become posthuman? Ageing and death, above all else, are the essential Transhumanist preoccupations. There's an irony in that, of course, because while most Transhumanists consider themselves to be adamantly secular, rejecting the 'supernatural' and placing their beliefs very much in the tradition of humanism, they share that concern with death and immortality with every religion that's ever existed.

The Transhumanist dream is that human life spans will become much longer – and that means longer periods of robust health, not merely additional years of decrepitude – until we ultimately attain immortality. For Transhumanists, that is so clearly a desirable goal that there is no reason to retain a sentimental attachment to our existing human bodies or way of life. Ultimately, in fact, we may have to leave those bodies altogether; even once they become as genetically perfect as we can possibly imagine, they may remain too vulnerable to violent accident for it to be safe for us to stay in them. Here too, in the notion that our physical bodies are peripheral to our existence as human beings, there are clearly echoes of religious belief.

Some Transhumanists see scientific advances as being incremental, continuing indefinitely into the future without necessarily accelerating. Others foresee posthuman status as arriving in a sudden, blinding moment – the Singularity. The term was originally invented to refer to the hypothetical instant when artificial intelligence first transcends human thought, enabling machines to pass not only beyond human understanding, but beyond human control, and thus ending humanity's role as the dominant species. The leading proponent of that idea is Ray Kurzweil, currently director of engineering at Google, whose book *The Singularity Is Near* was recommended by Dan Brown as further reading for *Inferno* fans. In the Transhumanist Singularity, however, it's the new, emergent breed of posthumans that will supplant the existing species.

And when Transhumanists say 'we' will become immortal, they really do mean us – not abstract future generations, but you and I, and others alive today. Or at least, they say they do, though sceptics – and, perhaps, readers of *Inferno* – can't help wondering whether they can be trusted. Perhaps the 'we' applies only to the scientists themselves, or to the elite in the affluent West; certainly it's hard to picture a moment when *all* humans suddenly become posthuman.

This is why Dan Brown's Bertrand Zobrist regards himself as making such a sacrifice. Although, assuming that he's the Transhumanist he claims to be, his goal is to extend human life spans to the point of immortality, he himself is suffering (permanent) death in order to make that possible. He calls himself 'the gateway to the Posthuman age', but he will not become posthuman himself. Hence his hubristic self-comparison to Martin Luther King, Jr, who in what's known as the 'I have been to the mountaintop' speech, spoke the night before he died of the desirability of longevity, while acknowledging that 'I may not get there with you'.

Leaving aside whether Zobrist's actions make all that much sense in terms of the plot of *Inferno* itself, and, for the moment, whether the views of this fictional character do in fact reflect those of actual Transhumanists, it's worth stressing that there is no intrinsic link between Transhumanism and Malthusian theories. Overpopulation is not an issue that's particularly addressed in Transhumanist writings, and Transhumanism does not in any sense present itself as a solution to rising population numbers, or indeed to any other current human problems.

WHO ARE THE TRANSHUMANISTS, AND WHERE DID THEY COME FROM?

Generally speaking, the Transhumanist movement is made up of responsible individuals—ethically accountable scientists, futurists, visionaries.

Elizabeth Sinskey, *Inferno* chapter 73

For as long as human beings have existed, we have directed at least part of our energy and attention towards what are now the two prime facets of Transhumanism – firstly using technological advances to ameliorate our living conditions in general, and our health in particular, and secondly searching for ways to overcome death and achieve eternal life.

The Babylonian *Epic of Gilgamesh*, for example, dating from approximately 1900 BC, is the story of Gilgamesh's perilous quest for immortality. Similarly, the ancient Egyptians furnished their tombs with food and other practical necessities in hope of ensuring an afterlife. It was also in Egypt, before the time of Christ, that alchemists started to explore the mutability of the material

This cuneiform tablet contains part of the Epic of Gilgamesh.

world in the hope of affecting not only inert substances – transmuting base metals into gold, for example – but also human nature.

The idea that humans are entitled – indeed authorised by God – to change and develop in any way they choose was beautifully expressed by the Renaissance philosopher Pico della Mirandola. In a text much cited by modern Transhumanists, the 1486 *Oration on the Dignity of Man*, he wrote that:

Pico della Mirandola

> *Neither a fixed abode nor a form that is thine alone nor any function peculiar to thyself have we given thee, Adam ... We have made thee neither of heaven nor Earth, neither mortal nor immortal, so that ... thou mayest fashion thyself in whatever shape thou shalt prefer.*

As described in Chapter Five of this book, Renaissance Florence saw an upsurge in humanist thought, influenced in particular by the Greek philosopher Gemistus Plethon. Similarly, the French Revolution inspired philosophers such as Nicolas de Condorcet and William Godwin to speculate about the future in what now read as proto-Transhumanist terms – and prompted Malthus to put pen to paper in response (see Chapter Seven).

Not until the twentieth century, however, did 'Transhumanism' first appear in print. In 1957, Julian Huxley – who was the brother of *Brave New World* author Aldous Huxley, and had long styled himself a humanist – argued in *New Bottles for New Wine* that 'The human species can, if it wishes, transcend itself – not just sporadically, an individual here in one way, an individual there in another way – but in its entirety, as humanity. We need a name for this new belief. Perhaps Transhumanism will serve.'

Fereidoun Esfandiary, the 'handsome Iranian man' featured in chapter 73 of *Inferno*, taught a course on 'New Concepts of the Human' at the New School in New York in the 1960s. He published *UpWingers: A Futurist Manifesto* in 1973, followed by a book called *Are You A Transhuman?* in 1989. The latter contained a questionnaire with the same title, which can be found in assorted versions online. As Dan Brown describes, Esfandiary changed his name to FM-2030, consisting of his initials and the year in which he hoped to celebrate his hundredth birthday, but he died, and was vitrified to await future reanimation, in 2000.

These days, as no one has exclusive rights to the term 'Transhumanist', there's no one, agreed definition as to what it exactly it means. Broadly speaking, common elements to the various outlines and manifestos that have been put forward include an enthusiastic and optimistic embrace of the potential for scientific advances to improve the individual and collective human condition; a belief that such changes are too inevitable to be thwarted by political or religious decrees; and at least some recognition that there are important ethical issues to address.

Largely, though not exclusively, Transhumanists are the actual scientists who are engaged in the relevant research. Many display a significant element of defiant self-justification, arguing that even if they don't do the work themselves, and governments attempt to outlaw it, it will happen anyway. As Gregory Stock put it in *Redesigning Humans: Our Inevitable Genetic Future* (2002), 'Policymakers sometimes think that they have a choice about whether germinal technologies will come into being. They do not.'

Many Transhumanists, and especially those who cohered to form the Extropy Institute in California in the 1990s, are libertarians, in that they dispute the right of governments to interfere in their work, and insist that they are entitled as individuals to do whatever they choose to their own bodies.

Others come from a more liberal perspective, explicitly acknowledging that their research does or will have social consequences, and that it should be available to all rather than some select or elite group. It's their views that are most closely reflected within the international Humanity+ organisation, which was established in 2008 to supercede what for ten years previously had been the World Transhumanist Association.

In *Inferno*, Elizabeth Sinskey makes it clear that she has no problem with Transhumanists *per se*. She expands upon the summation quoted on p.180, however, to say that 'as in many movements, there exists a small but militant faction ... [of] apocalyptic thinkers who believe the end is coming and that someone needs to take drastic action to save the future of the species.' If such real-life Bertrand Zobrists do exist, they remain as yet invisible to the naked eye.

WHAT DOES THE TRANSHUMANIST FUTURE HOLD?

Bertrand had boundless hope for mankind. He ... believed [that] in the span of several generations, our species would become a different animal entirely – genetically enhanced to be healthier, smarter, stronger, even more compassionate.

Sienna Brooks, *Inferno* chapter 73

The Transhumanist vision of the future is fundamentally Utopian. Not only will death cease to exist, but humans will become so downright *wise* that they'll be able to solve any resultant social or material problems.

The basic Transhumanist trajectory goes that human life spans will become longer and longer, with a guarantee of lasting good health. We're already used to the idea that if, for example, a hip or knee joint becomes painfully unsuitable for use, we can replace it. Transhumanists believe that it will soon become possible not only to 'regrow' such faulty parts – and organs as well – but also to provide even better artificial and not necessarily organic substitutes. The very process that causes ageing in individual cells – and thus entire organisms – will also be halted. Already, according to nanoscientist Robert A Freitas Jr, 'almost all … deaths are, in principle, medically preventable'. Effective immortality, Transhumanists believe, lies within our grasp.

More crucially still, there's no reason for us to remain within the existing parameters. If we take human beings simply to be the imperfect products of evolution, adapted to operate within specific conditions, many of our original specifications may no longer remain relevant. Thus for example Nick Bostrom, of the Future of Humanity Institute, argues that the humanoid ape that first stood upright on the African savannah had not only to be physically able to hunt for food, but also to carry out all its mental and bodily functions on the amount of food that was readily available. For modern human beings – affluent ones at any rate – acquiring food requires the expenditure of much less energy, and it would be straightforward for us to eat enough to fuel much greater mental activity. Similarly, perhaps the reason why we find it difficult to concentrate for extended periods is because we originally needed to be alert at all times to everything that was going on around us. Now, in the safety of our cities, humans may be free to develop our brain power to the point where we will become posthumans.

What exactly that means – what life might actually look like – is hard to pin down. Transhumanists such as Bostrom rhapsodise about us developing entirely new emotions, and creating entirely new art forms. What those might be and in what sense they'd be 'better' than those we currently have, by definition we don't know.

HOW THE HELL DID THEY DO THAT?

> Langdon had no idea what germ-line manipulation was, but it had an ominous ring.

Inferno, chapter 41

As every Dan Brown fan knows, unsuspected avenues are always liable to open up in front of even the mildest-mannered symbologist and lead to places unknown. For the moment, though, Transhumanists talk in terms of there being three principal highways to the future: genetic engineering, nanotechnology and information technology.

The first of those, genetic engineering, is perhaps the most familiar, and provides the central theme in *Inferno*. Consequent initially upon the discovery of DNA, and developed via the mapping of the human and other genomes, it is also the most controversial, being so closely tied in with notions of 'playing God'. In the short term, the basic idea is that the more we know about the precise effects of having a specific genetic make-up, the more it will become possible to pre-empt potential problems as well as to cure actual diseases. We've already reached the point where it's possible to buy a map of your own genes for around $100, and to thus take unprecedented control over your own health prospects. The most relevant technique in terms of individual treatment is 'somatic cell gene modification', in which new segments of DNA are inserted into, say, the blood or liver cells of a specific person, to treat some medical condition. From there, however, it's a small step to Bertrand Zobrist's speciality, germ-line manipulation

– yes, it really does exist, albeit usually under slightly different names, such as 'germline gene modification' – in which DNA is added to sperm or unfertilised eggs and thus becomes part of the relevant person's inheritable genetic make-up.

So far, scientists have only been able to identify a limited number of medical conditions that can be attributed to a single specific, and thus potentially alterable, genetic variation, and successful treatments remain rare. In his book *An Optimist's Tour of the Future*, Mark Stevenson details the case of the eighteen-year-old Jesse Gelsinger, who had the rare metabolic disorder known as ornithine transcarbamylase (OTC) deficiency. Although Jesse's own condition was manageable rather than life-threatening, he volunteered as a guinea pig to help develop future treatments for newborns, for whom OTC deficiency frequently proves fatal. Jesse was injected with a genetically engineered 'adeno-virus' designed to alter the relevant cells, but died when his body rejected the virus and went into shock. That was back in 1999, and has been taken by many scientists as an indication that creating artificial viruses – the approach that's used by Bertrand Zobrist in *Inferno* – may be an ineffective and dangerous way to administer treatments.

The second string to the Transhumanist bow, nanotechnology, is concerned with what's seen as the all but infinite potential of engineering on an infinitesimally small scale. As in, working in nanometres, each of which is a billionth of a metre across – a human hair, by way of comparison, is approximately eighty thousand nanometres in diameter. Working at that level would make it possible to rearrange individual atoms in whichever combinations we choose, and thus effectively create whatever matter we need. The result has been described as 'a world without scarcity'.

Nanotechnology is not a single discipline with a single application, but an approach that proponents believe can be turned to almost anything, including the production of unlimited supplies of food and fuel. They talk of 'molecular manufacturing' in 'nanofactories', and as far as they're concerned the beauty of the system is that it's self-replicating – as each nanofactory can be set to build whatever we want, they can therefore build more and more nanofactories.

At this point in the discussion, the dreaded spectre of 'grey goo' rears its head. What if we inadvertently start a chain reaction in which an unstoppable stream of tiny nanofactories churns our entire planet into an indistinguishable mass of grey goo?

The 1966 movie Fantastic Voyage *depicts an over-simplified version of nanotechnology, in which a surgeon is miniaturised and injected into the human bloodstream in a miniature submarine.*

It's the associated field of nanomedicine that is particularly relevant to the Transhumanist project. Within, say, the next couple of decades, it's argued that a new breed of nanorobots will enable us to do away with such crude interventions as surgery and radiotherapy. Instead, we'll be able to inject little robotic doctors into affected areas of the body, where they can target cancerous cells, for example, with invisible but deadly precision.

The third and final element of the Transhumanist trinity is that science-fiction staple, the superbrain. Or, rather, the inevitable trajectory of developments in information technology towards the creation of artificial intelligence that unarguably surpasses current human thinking power. For a certain kind of scientist, particularly those with a strong predisposition towards determinism, there's nothing much wrong with the world that the ability to process colossal quantities of data at mind-boggling speed couldn't cure. The moment will arrive – and this is what advocates like Ray Kurzweil call the Singularity – when it becomes not only essential but actually unpreventable that the computers take over. We may not currently be able to imagine the benefits to humans that will ensue, both individually and collectively, but rest assured, they say, there are *lots*.

There's a subsidiary strand to this talk of coming advances in computing. The more we can understand the workings of our brains, and the more we can create computers that model and ultimately surpass those workings, the closer the connections may become between artificial and organic intelligence. Thus we may become able to replace parts of our own brains with more efficient and longer-lasting manufactured components; to add entirely new parts and thus expand our powers in unimaginable directions; and by growing ever more integrated with our computers make it possible to migrate to cyberbodies or some other form of permanent storage. Always assuming, *Matrix* fans, that we have not already done so.

A Stairway to Heaven?

'You taught me how man makes himself immortal'

Dante, writing of Brunetto Latini, Canto XV, *Inferno*

Woody Allen famously wrote that 'I don't want to achieve immortality through my work, I want to achieve it by not dying'. Ever the optimists, Transhumanists hope to achieve the best of both worlds: they plan, through their work, not to die.

In 1900, the average life expectancy for someone born in the United States was 46 years for a male, 48 for a female. By 2011, those figures had reached 76 and 81 respectively. In other words, on average, for each year that went by, life expectancy rose by almost four extra months. Transhumanists argue that there's no need to imagine a 'natural' limit to human longevity – say, a maximum life span of just over a century. Instead, we might attain 'escape velocity', in which for each year that you live, your anticipated life span will increase by *more* than a year, meaning you'll never actually reach your predicted date of death. To take a simple example, let's imagine the day scientists finally find a 'cure' for cancer. As of that moment, average life expectancy will rise by perhaps five years. And as each such new discovery is made, your projected death will recede further into the future – the longer you manage to live, the longer you will continue to live thereafter.

How exactly we are going to become immortal, you may not be surprised to learn, no one knows. Some Transhumanists believe we'll find a 'magic bullet' that puts an end to ageing. Current hopes centre on the discovery that each time a cell in your body divides, you lose a little piece of DNA known as a telemere. The progressive loss of those telemeres creates a 'ticking clock', counting down to the point where you run out of telemeres, your cells can no longer divide, and you die. By that reckoning, an enzyme known as telomerase, obtainable from a protozoan organism found in freshwater ponds, may be the 'Fountain of Youth'. Use telomerase to top up your telemeres, the theory goes, and your body will never grow old. The trouble is, telomerase has also been strongly associated with the growth of cancerous tumours...

Other scientists believe that we'll develop a much broader armoury of techniques and treatments, as described throughout this chapter, which, incorporated into a carefully managed programme of control, repair and replacement – including with prosthetic and cybernetic spare parts – will prolong our lives indefinitely. As the MIT-based Marvin Minsky, one of the apostles of artificial intelligence, puts it: 'In the end, we will find ways to replace every part of the body and brain, and thus repair all the defects that make our lives so brief.' Which does of course beg the age-old question, if you take a broomstick, and first replace the brush, and then replace the handle, is it still the same broomstick? Or to put it another way, will I still be me? Will you still be you? And if not, who will we be?

UTOPIA OR DYSTOPIA?

Legalised genetic enhancements would immediately create a world of haves and have-nots.

Robert Langdon, *Inferno*, chapter 67

Transhumanists and the ideas they espouse have long attracted suspicion and opposition. Objections to their vision of the future range from the purely practical – are the envisaged technological advances actually possible to achieve? – to the political – will they result in further inequality, and exacerbate the rich-poor divide? – and from the philosophical – would we still be human? – to the religious – is the Transhumanist programme amoral, godless, or even just plain evil? Invited by *Foreign Policy* magazine to name the 'most dangerous idea in the world' in 2004, for example, political scientist Francis Fukuyama described the 'tempting offerings' of biotechnology as coming at a 'frightful moral cost'.

Czech playwright Karel Capek invented the 'robot' in his 1920 play R.U.R.

Fukuyama's article was written at a time when the United States was in a moral panic about the implications of genetic engineering, with especial reference to stem cell and embryo research. The American Association for the Advancement of Science had called in 2000 for a complete halt to work on what it called 'inheritable genetic modifications', which also encompassed human cloning and germ-line modification. President George W Bush subsequently appointed a Council on Bioethics, largely dominated by conservative Christians, which in its 2003 report *Beyond Therapy* accepted 'that technology will be available to significantly retard the process of aging, of both body and mind, and... that this technology will be widely available and widely used'.

The chairman of the Council on Bioethics, Leon Kass, who characterises himself as a humanist, has become a particular bugbear for Transhumanists. He coined the notion in 1997 that in certain 'crucial cases', we should take 'repugnance' as our moral compass: 'repugnance is the emotional expression of deep wisdom, beyond reason's power fully to articulate it'. In one particularly memorable phrase, he described cloning as 'a profound defilement of our given nature as procreative beings ... Shallow are the souls that have forgotten how to shudder.'

Nothing could be more calculated to get a scientist's goat than the suggestion that some issues lie beyond rational discussion, and should be settled instead on the basis of gut feelings. Transhumanists take exception to the view that their vision of the future represents some new and unacceptable departure, rather than a logical continuation of the way human development has always worked. They argue that there's no qualitative difference between the earliest human scientific accomplishments and those that might become available to us tomorrow. Discovering that meat becomes more digestible when it's cooked over a fire, for example, enabled us to eat more – enough to provide energy for larger brains, which we duly evolved. If it was morally acceptable for us to devise lenses and manufacture stylish Plume Paris glasses in order to see better, why does it become wrong if we seek to create better eyes instead?

Even if we have not yet become posthuman, we are already products of an ongoing process that will take us there. As Sienna Brooks puts it in chapter 102 of *Inferno*, 'genetic engineering is not an acceleration of the evolutionary process. It is the natural course of events! ... It was evolution that created Bertrand Zobrist. His superior intellect was the product of the very process Darwin described.'

All of which can veer perilously close to a blithe indifference to the very existence of moral problems and dilemmas. While paying lip service to the idea that of course we need to talk things through, certain Transhumanist writings appear to be imbued with the attitude that it's all going to happen anyway, whether you like it or not, and that if I don't do it myself, someone else will go ahead and do it instead, and since they're not as clever as me I'd better get on with it quick.

GREAT EXPECTATIONS – BUT ARE THEY EQUAL?

The conflict between rationalism and religion has been raging long enough that it's a familiar battleground for scientists, who can argue that it's possible to operate on an ethical basis even if you don't believe in a supreme deity. Many are on shakier ground when it comes to taking responsibility for the political consequences of their work. Whether the benefits of future biotech will be shared by humanity as a whole – and if so, how – is not at all clear. Life expectancy may be rising throughout the world, but that doesn't mean that everyone has access to the latest drugs and medical techniques. Why should we assume that things will become any more equal when the first posthumans begin to appear? Is that not more likely, as the handsome academic Robert Langdon characteristically intuits, to instigate the ultimate divide between the haves and have-nots?

Not surprisingly, the echoes in genetic engineering of eugenics, and notions of creating a super-race, strike a resonant chord in Germany. Back in 1991, that country's Embryo Protection Law specified a five-year prison sentence for anyone attempting germ-line manipulation. The German minister of justice described the law as designed to 'exclude even the slightest chance for programmes aimed at the so-called improvement of humans'.

While it's often taken for granted that the 'we' who might experience the impact of the Transhumanist programme live in the wealthy West, such countries tend to be democracies that are open to ethical debates, and where governments are not free to disregard the moral or religious scruples of their citizens. Arguably, however, in the light of twentieth-century history, genetic engineering on a mass scale is more likely to take place under authoritarian rule. Perhaps in China, for example, where the 'One Child' policy has already re-shaped the genetic make-up of a billion-strong population…

Transhumanism in Sci-Fi

This all feels like science fiction to me at the moment.

Elizabeth Sinskey, *Inferno* chapter 102

It's only to be expected that science fiction, so often concerned with possible human futures, should be filled with stark prefigurations – and even, here and there, optimistic predictions – of the elements of Transhumanism. As well as the novels below, it's worth mentioning films and TV series including *Star Trek* – any existing human attempting to understand new, posthuman emotions will surely be reminded of the struggles of that Vulcan naïf, Mr Spock; *The Matrix*, in which humans have been confined to virtual storage by sentient machines; and *Dr Who*, in which the Cybermen correspond quite closely to one potential posthuman possibility.

Frankenstein, or the Modern Prometheus Mary Shelley, 1818. Prometheus being Dr Frankenstein himself, the scientist with a lack of ethical restraints, and his melancholy creature being the classic example of why just because you can create life in the lab, it doesn't mean that you should. Mary Shelley was the daughter of William Godwin, to whose ideas Malthus responded in his *Essay*.

The Island of Dr Moreau H G Wells, 1896. At the end of the nineteenth century, the science-fiction pioneer depicted a world in which scientists seek to improve on human biology by creating what Leon Kass (see p.191) would surely agree are 'repugnant' human–animal hybrids.

Last and First Men Olaf Stapledon, 1930. An ambitious bid to write an entire future history of humanity. Things rather go wrong after the Third Men invent a giant brain, which first takes over the world and then uses genetic engineering to remodel human beings altogether.

Brave New World Aldous Huxley, 1932. His brother may have given the world the word 'Transhumanism', but Aldous's new world, which features bionic engineering on a global scale, is far indeed from a posthuman Utopia, and has been cited by Francis Fukuyama as a definitive warning.

At The Mountains of Madness H P Lovecraft, 1936. Master of eldritch if not always entirely coherent horror, H P Lovecraft was not really a science-fiction author; his concerns lay with the unspeakably remote past. He deserves inclusion here, though, for his menagerie of subterranean 'chthonic' monsters – most notoriously, Cthulhu. That the word features in Bertrand Zobrist's vocabulary can safely be ascribed to Lovecraft's influence.

Do Androids Dream of Electric Sheep? Philip K Dick, 1968. In Dick's dark world, best known from the movie adaptation *Blade Runner*, it takes an intricate empathy test to distinguish an android from a human – and even the androids don't know which they are.

Neuromancer William Gibson, 1984. In the original 'cyberpunk' novel, published at the dawn of the personal computer era, Gibson envisaged cyborgs stalking through a computer-generated hell, and was hailed by one reviewer as the 'Dante of the coming age'.

3001: The Final Odyssey Arthur C Clarke, 1997. The final novel of the *Odyssey* series describes a world in which each inhabitant is fitted with a 'BrainCap', inextricably intertwined into their organic brains, which makes them part human, part computer – in the Transhumanist sense, posthuman.

WHERE DO BERTRAND ZOBRIST AND DAN BROWN FIT INTO ALL THIS?

Zobrist's views on overpopulation seem to endorse killing off people. His ideas on Transhumanism and overpopulation seem to be in conflict, don't they?

Robert Langdon, *Inferno* chapter 51

With the necessary caveat that Transhumanists are a varied bunch, Dan Brown's *Inferno* provides a reasonably fair depiction of their beliefs and aspirations. It's worth noting, however, that although the novel's Machiavellian archvillain Bertrand Zobrist is a self-proclaimed Transhumanist, neither Zobrist nor Brown say much that's at all specific about the actual Transhumanist vision of the future. Instead, Zobrist's obsession is with the current human situation, and specifically what he regards as the crisis of overpopulation. While he unleashes his genetically engineered virus in order to buy time for the Transhumanist future to arrive, what Sienna Brooks describes as a 'Transhumanist Black Death' has little to do with Transhumanism itself. You don't, on the whole, find Transhumanists advocating the mass culling of humanity.

As suggested in Chapter Seven of this book, one can't help suspecting that Zobrist shares his apocalyptic Malthusian preoccupations with his creator. Whether Dan Brown also has Transhumanist sympathies is less clear. In his messianic self-importance, Zobrist might arguably be intended as a parody of the self-righteous strand apparent in some Transhumanist literature. Much as Zobrist describes himself as the 'glorious savior', so with certain Transhumanists their sheer faith in their agenda, and in their own ethical probity, gives Transhumanism all the fervour of an alternative religion.

In his essay *For Enhancing People*, for example, Ronald Bailey announces that genetic enhancements 'will enable people to become more virtuous', while Nick Bostrom, in his article *Why I Want to be a Posthuman When I Grow Up*, talks about religious believers being 'already accustomed to the prospect of an extremely radical transformation into a kind of posthuman being'. Physics professor Frank Tipler has taken things further, finding common ground between Transhumanism and his Christian faith. His 1994 book *The Physics of Immortality* argues that 'we humans shall have life after death, in an abode that closely resembles the Heaven of the great world religions'. And where there's a Heaven, as Dante could certainly tell you, there's always likely to be a Hell.

PART THREE

INFERNAL LOCATIONS

A Hard Day's Journey

The dramatic events depicted in Dan Brown's *Inferno* take place in March. The action begins in the middle of the night, as Robert Langdon begins to awaken from unconsciousness. He has no idea where he is, let alone why he's there. Almost nothing he sees, it will eventually transpire, is what it seems to be. Of one thing, though, he can be certain – the 'illuminated skyline' outside his window is that of Florence.

All too soon, Langdon and Sienna Brooks are hurtling through the streets of the city. By the time they've left her apartment and are riding towards the Porta Romana, it is early morning. In the hectic chase that follows, they pass by and through several of Florence's principal monuments and landmarks.

When the fugitives enter the Baptistery, it's still 'several hours' before opening time, which is 1pm. The high-speed train to Venice takes two hours, and they arrive at St Mark's in 'late afternoon'.

The flying time from Venice to Istanbul is two hours, and on top of that the difference in time zones makes it an hour later in Istanbul. When Langdon arrives, 'night had fallen on the ancient Byzantine capital'. He remarks that the great Byzantine church of 'Hagia Sophia closes at sunset', but it is specially opened for his visit. By the time everything is over, it is the middle of the night again. The entire story of *Inferno* has taken twenty-four hours.

Even during the most hair-raising episodes of that long day, Langdon and Brown between them manage to provide Sienna, and the readers of the novel, with a narrated tour of the historic and cultural highlights of those three cities.

In the next two chapters of this book, we set out to put some extra flesh on those bones. If *Inferno* has inspired you to follow in the footsteps of Robert Langdon and Sienna Brooks – or even those of Bertrand Zobrist – now read on…

CHAPTER TEN

Florence

The desperate, day-long chase at the heart of Dan Brown's *Inferno* begins when Sienna Brooks and Robert Langdon escape from the **hospital** where Vayentha – complete with black leather motorcycle suit, close-cropped spiked hair, and silenced weapon – has tried to do her worst. They head first to **Sienna's apartment** in 'a dingy residential neighbourhood' somewhere in the southern suburbs of the city. When that apartment in turn comes under siege, this time from men in black uniforms led by an icy-eyed agent with an impressive umlaut, they escape again. Soon they are gliding on Sienna's Trike in the early morning light along the **Viale Niccolo Machiavelli**, 'the most graceful of all Florentine avenues', as it descends in a series of generous S-curves through a lush green landscape of hedges and trees towards the River Arno. They are heading for the historical centre of Florence on the other side.

As they approach the **Porta Romana**, a well-preserved city gate dating from the early fourteenth century, they run into a traffic jam caused by a police barricade. 'That can't be for us', thinks Langdon in some amazement; but it is. Sienna quickly pulls the Trike off the road so that they can continue their escape on foot, climbing over a wall into the Boboli Gardens.

Bypassing the police roadblock through the gardens would lead them to the Palazzo Pitti, from where they could cross over the bridge into the heart of the old city.

The extensive **Boboli Gardens (1)** are among the most beautiful in Italy. They were created in the middle of the sixteenth century for Cosimo I de Medici, ruler of Florence and all Tuscany, by Niccolò Tribolo. A brilliant hydraulic engineer, Tribolo made creative use of fountains and cascades amid the maze of pathways. Later that same century, Giorgio Vasari embellished the gardens still further. Now, as Langdon and Sienna make their way across those same gardens, they realise that they are being tracked by a drone overhead.

The couple dash into the back of the **Palazzo Pitti (2)**, which became the official seat of the Medici dynasty in 1549, in the time of Cosimo I and following his move from the Palazzo Vecchio. These days it's a fabulous museum, containing one of the finest collections of paintings in all Italy, including works by Raphael, Rubens and Titian. Sadly, Langdon and Sienna have no time for any of that; they discover that their way out through the front is blocked by armed police. Making a misleading feint towards the costume gallery, they race out the back, the way they came in, and run down the slope past a statue of an obese naked dwarf astride a giant turtle.

'This can't be where he's taking us', exclaims Sienna to herself, as they race towards the **Buontalenti Grotto (3)**. Stalactites hang over the grotto's gaping entrance, while the walls of the chamber beyond are 'oozing' and 'melting', and also 'morphing into shapes' that to the fearful Sienna look like 'half-buried humanoids extruding from the walls as if being consumed by the stone'. The whole thing looks like a scene out of Botticelli's *Mappa dell'Inferno*, she thinks. Although that description accurately captures the creepy and disgusting atmosphere of the place, that was far from the intention of

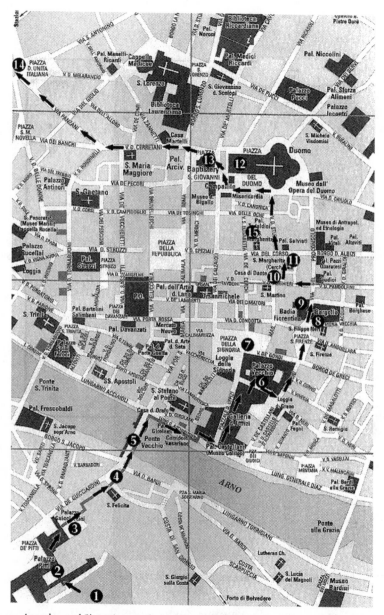

Langdon and Sienna's route through Florence; map courtesy of Blue Guides.

The Buontalenti Grotto in the Boboli Gardens.

the grotto's creator, the architect and stage designer Bernardo Buontalenti, late in the sixteenth century. At that time, it would have been running with water and hung with dripping moss, the statues and reliefs round the walls serving to create a happy merging of man with nature.

Langdon and Brooks manage to avoid detection in the grotto – knowing a bit of *dim mak* is always handy in a crisis – but they realise that there's no chance of escape if they venture out into the open and attempt to cross the river over the nearby Ponte Vecchio. Faced with the police, the soldiers and the drone all in action, not to mention Vayentha and her spiked hair, the pair trick their way into the **Vasari Corridor (4)**. The corridor was built by Giorgio Vasari for Francesco de Medici in 1565 as a way for him to move from the Palazzo Vecchio, the seat of government, through the Uffizi, the 'offices' which then housed the bureaucracy and is now the famous art gallery, and over the River Arno to the family home at the Palazzo Pitti. It was a convenient passage in wet weather, and ideal for anyone elderly or in a wheelchair, but it also had the added bonus of keeping the Medici off the streets, where they were liable to be assassinated.

This walkway, which runs for well over half a mile through the city, makes clever use of existing features, including the **Ponte Vecchio (5)**, the old stone bridge, which is lined with houses. The corridor simply adds another storey to the existing buildings and passes unnoticed. One change was required, however. Before the corridor was built, the buildings on the

Looking out along the Ponte Vecchio from the Vasari Corridor.

bridge were occupied by butchers and the smell could be unpleasant; these were removed and replaced with goldsmiths who remain there till this day. Few people know about the Vasari Corridor, and tours cost a fortune, but it is worth it for the fun, the sense of doing something secret, for the marvellous views along the Arno – Mussolini had large windows installed at vantage points so that a visiting Hitler could enjoy the scene – and for the many self-portraits by artists that hang along its walls.

Eventually, Langdon and Sienna emerge from the Vasari Corridor in the fortress-like **Palazzo Vecchio (6)**, which was built at the very end of the thirteenth century to house the priori, the topmost tier of officials governing Florence. Thus Dante, who was elected a prior, held office in this very place. Nowadays it contains several museums and halls and chambers that can take many hours to explore, including the **Hall of the Five Hundred** with the enigmatic words 'cerca trova' – seek and you will find – written on a banner in a battle scene painted by Vasari. Sundry stairways, passageways, attics and tunnels make it the perfect place for Sienna and Langdon to evade their pursuers for some time.

Langdon, who has of course been here many times before, knows all there is know about its secret passageways. He proceeds to demonstrate his erudition by whiling away twenty pages of *Inferno* in giving the reader a tour while he and Sienna are being chased. Starting through the corridor that opens up behind

Dante's death mask plays a crucial role in Robert Langdon's search for clues.

the Armenia panel in the **Hall of Geographical Maps**, they then head into the cupboard in the room of architectural models, down the Duke of Athens stairway, and at some point in between manage to get up into the attic. That's when the poor pursuing Vayentha falls for a full three seconds and splats very much dead far below. All these areas are open to visitors, including Francesco de Medici's mysterious **Studiolo** where he practised alchemy and other dark arts. There's also **Dante's death mask**, of course, always assuming that they have put it back since Langdon stole it.

Outside, the **Piazza della Signoria (7)**, the great square overlooked by wonderful Renaissance statues that include Michelangelo's **David**, is where the scaffold was built for **Savonarola** who was hanged and burned for heresy and generally making a nuisance of himself. Among his most devoted followers was Botticelli, who probably watched as Savonarola

Michelangelo's David.

was reduced to cinders; this was at about the time that Botticelli was working on his *Map of Hell* to illustrate Dante's *Inferno*.

Slipping out a small side door of the Palazzo Vecchio into the Via della Ninna, Langdon and Sienna – now disguised as punk rockers, by the way – then head north along the Via dei Leoni. They pass between the **Bargello (8)** on the right – an old seat of government, later a prison infamous for its tortures, now a museum noted for its superb collection of Florentine Renaissance sculpture – and the **Badia (9)** on the left. Nowadays the Badia is a very quiet place, home to the Monastic Fraternity of Jerusalem who give themselves up to silent prayer and contemplation. It was founded as a Benedictine abbey in the tenth century; Dante mentions the tolling of its bells in his *Divine Comedy*. And, of course, it was from the tall spire of the Badia that the Shade, aka Bertrand Zobrist, leaped to his death at the very start of *Inferno*.

Continuing north and then west into the Via Dante Alighieri, Langdon leads Sienna to the **Casa di Dante (10)**. This is not Dante's actual house, as Langdon explains to Sienna – it's a twentieth-century reconstruction of a thirteenth-century house – but a museum that holds a collection of maps, models and reconstructions giving an impression of Florence in Dante's time. Langdon has come here because he has been given a clue, and hopes the shop will have a copy of Dante's *Divine Comedy* to find out what it means. But the Casa di Dante is closed.

Just north along the narrow street running north, however, is **Santa Margherita de Cerchi (11)**, popularly known as Dante's Church because it was his family's parish church. It contains the Portinari family tomb, and some believe that Beatrice Portinari herself, the great love of Dante's life, is buried here. Certainly an inscription says so, and a basket near the tomb overflows with handwritten messages from the lovelorn asking Beatrice for her intervention.

Dan Brown is wrong, however, in writing that here in this church Dante, at the age of nine, first laid eyes on Beatrice. There is one source and one source only that tells us where Dante and Beatrice first met, and that is Boccaccio's life of Dante, which says they met at the Portinari family home, which is round the corner at the **Palazzo Portinari Salviati** at 6 Via del Corso.

Dante and Virgil (the cloaked figures on the left) visit Satan in Hell, depicted on a mosaic on the Baptistery ceiling.

Crossing the Via del Corso and walking north along the Via dello Studio, Langdon and Sienna come up against the flank of the **Duomo (12)**, the great cathedral of Santa Maria del Fiore, crowned by the largest masonry dome in the world, the work of Brunelleschi. Skirting round the Duomo's **campanile**, the huge bell tower built by Dante's friend Giotto, they are now standing at the front of the cathedral. Still following his clues, Langdon is looking west for the Gates of Paradise.

The **Baptistery (13)** stands before them, and they walk across the piazza to its magnificent **east doors**. Commissioned to appease the wrath of God and to avert a future plague, these were cast in bronze by Ghiberti and described by Michelangelo as 'the Gates of Paradise'. The doors have been secretly left open for Langdon and Sienna by the corpulent and now deceased Ignazio Busoni, and, unnoticed, the two go inside. One of the oldest buildings in Florence, the octagonal Baptistery was built in the sixth or seventh century, and its marvellous mosaic ceiling, some of the best mosaic work anywhere in Italy, was done in the thirteenth century. We can be sure, therefore, that Dante himself, who was baptised here – as were most other Florentine children – gazed up at this very same ceiling as an infant, and would have seen its horrific images of Satan and the damned. About a century after Dante's death, and as a tribute to him from the city that exiled him and would have burned him at the stake, his figure, along with that of Virgil, was added to the mosaic.

Meanwhile Langdon has found another clue, which demands that he leaves Florence undetected and as quickly as possible. Assuming that the airport is being watched, he and Sienna, who have now been joined by a very itchy man sporting Plume Paris glasses, do the sensible thing and take a taxi along the Via Panzani to the **Santa Maria Novella railway station (14)**, where they board a high-speed train to Venice.

Before we follow Robert Langdon and Sienna Brooks to Venice and beyond, we can briefly look ahead to the moment when Langdon eventually returns to Florence for a good night's sleep. He stays at his favourite hotel, the one he mentions at the end of *The Da Vinci Code*, and here in *Inferno* describes as 'Florence's elegant' **Hotel Brunelleschi (15)**. Quite possibly the appeal of the hotel to Langdon lies more in its history than in its elegance, for it incorporates a high round stone Byzantine tower, which means it is the oldest standing thing in the city, and in the cellars of the tower are the remains of an ancient church and, older than that, a Roman baths. The view from its highest rooms towards Brunelleschi's dome is spectacular.

✳ CHAPTER ELEVEN ✳

𝔙enice and 𝔍stanbul

The story of *Inferno* could have played itself out entirely in Florence; that would have seemed natural enough. Instead it moves from Florence to Venice and then to Constantinople, present-day Istanbul. In moving this way, from West to East, the story is retracing in reverse two great events.

The first is the Black Death epidemic, which began somewhere deep in Asia, travelled westwards to Constantinople and the Black Sea, and was carried from there by Genoese galleys to Italy – first to Venice, then to Sicily and Genoa, and finally to Florence in 1348. It then spread throughout the whole of Europe, claiming as many as one out of every two human lives, and in some places even more than that.

The second is the stimulus to the Renaissance that was provided by Byzantine civilisation before Constantinople fell to the Ottoman Turks. The Byzantines had long made themselves felt; the mosaics at the Basilica of St Mark in Venice are entirely the work of craftsmen from Constantinople, while the early mosaics at the Baptistery in Florence were made by Byzantine-trained craftsmen from Venice.

The whole back catalogue of ancient Greek and Roman civilisation that was preserved by the Byzantines – and indeed, to a great extent, was still actually *lived* by the Byzantines – was brought by them to Italy, and especially to Florence, in those last days before they lost their world to Mehmet the Conqueror and the armies of Islam.

VENICE

The clue that Robert Langdon had found at the Baptistery in Florence started off as a verse of Dante, but soon became something else, a message written by Bertrand Zobrist himself. 'Seek the treacherous doge', his words began, 'who severed the heads from horses'. To Langdon this pointed to **Venice**.

'Kneel within the gilded mouseion of the holy wisdom', the message continued, which suggested to Langdon the **Basilica of St Mark**, the state church of Venice and the chapel of the doges, its interior luminous with mosaics and gold. That rich decoration earned the basilica the name of the *chiesa d'oro*, the golden church. Surmounting the central doorway of the church are the four bronze horses that were sent to Venice by Doge Enrico Dandolo in 1204, following his conquest of Constantinople, where they had stood in the Hippodrome.

Santa Lucia railway station stands at the far end of the **Grand Canal**. From there, thinks Langdon, there is nothing more pleasant if you have the time than to take the #1 *vaporetto* along the whole of its length, sitting up front in the open air, watching the churches and palaces pass by.

Langdon, however, does not have the time. He hires a high-speed water limousine, and he and Sienna, along with a fidgety fellow called Ferris with whom they somehow got fixed up back at the Baptistery in Florence, surge off towards the Basilica

The interior of the Basilica of St Mark in Venice.

of St Mark, standing close to where the Grand Canal opens onto the lagoon and where cruise ships arrive in monotonous succession from the open sea.

Langdon and Sienna quickly move through the body of the church and go up to the balcony to take a close look at the bronze horses – only to glance down at the piazza below and see a commotion of black-uniformed soldiers. Once again Sienna and Langdon are on the run, this time scurrying down into the crypt that contains the bones of St Mark himself.

Up to this point the clues have seemed to match Venice and St Mark's. Suddenly however new associations rearrange Langdon's thoughts; he turns to Sienna, telling her 'I made a mistake'. Sienna looks at him and turns pale. Are we in the wrong place, she wants to know. '"Sienna", Langdon whispers, feeling ill. "We're in the wrong country."'

And so off they go again, within moments, to Istanbul – albeit now estranged and flying separately. The whole of the action in *Inferno* takes place over the course of a sleepless day and night, but the visit by Langdon and Sienna to Venice sets a touristic record, quicker even than the tour groups disembarking from the unending queue of cruise liners. It cannot have lasted more than an hour and a half.

ISTANBUL

What Langdon has realised is that 'the gilded mouseion of the holy wisdom' refers to the Byzantine church of **Hagia Sophia** in **Istanbul**; Hagia Sophia is the Greek for holy wisdom. He also realises that the doge in question, Enrico Dandolo, was buried not in Venice but in Constantinople; in fact when Dandolo died in Constantinople in 1205 he was placed in a sarcophagus in the south gallery of the Hagia Sophia. So this is where the clue tells Langdon to come and kneel and listen for 'the sounds of trickling water' and 'follow deep into the sunken palace'.

Langdon's plane arrives at Ataturk airport. From there, he is driven along the highway, named for John F Kennedy, which runs along the Sea of Marmara and through the ancient Land Walls of Constantinople. Constantinople, Istanbul, Byzantium, Stamboul: for 2,500 years this city has stood under different names and different rulers by the narrow waterway of the Bosphorus that separates Europe and Asia. In AD 324, Constantine made it the capital of the Roman Empire. When the Western Empire collapsed in AD 476, the era of the Byzantine Empire began, and Constantinople became the centre of the civilised world. For a thousand years the city held off attacks by Arabs, Barbarians and Seljuk Turks, preserving and developing within her the highest attainments of Greek culture, and surviving just long enough to transmit the Classical and Byzantine achievements to a re-ordered and re-awakening Western Europe.

The end came on a May night in 1453, when a crescent of fire embraced the walls as the overwhelming Ottoman army of Sultan Mehmet prepared for the morning kill. The last emperor, named Constantine like the first, gathered his followers in Hagia Sophia, the most magnificent church in Christendom, to celebrate a final mass amid sobs, wailings and cries of Kyrie eleison. Calling 'God forbid that I should

The interior of Hagia Sophia in Istanbul.

215

live an Emperor without an Empire! As the city falls, I will fall with it!', Constantine rode out against the Turks, and was immediately cut down.

Langdon is driven past the gaping windows of the Byzantine sea palace of Bucoleon, and round the headland of the old city until he and others – now including the icy-eyed man, along with his umlaut – are deposited in the park between the Blue Mosque and the Hagia Sophia. By this time everyone is on the same side, trying to save mankind from the great cull.

'Hovering beneath the water, an undulating bubble of transparent plastic containing a gelatinous, yellow-brown liquid'... the Yerebatan Saray cistern in Istanbul.

'Not so much a building as a mountain', the **Hagia Sophia** strikes Langdon with 'the staggering force of its enormity'. In AD 532 the Emperor Justinian gathered thousands of workers and a hundred of the finest masters and architects from all over the ancient world to build a church that would rival in size and beauty any building constructed to that day. Five years later at the inauguration ceremony, Justinian, in reference to the fabled Temple in Jerusalem, cried out, 'O Solomon, I have surpassed thee!' He had achieved more than that. The impressive interior of Hagia Sophia has only been equalled in the succeeding 1,500 years by the cathedral of Chartres.

The beauty of the interior lies in the enormous space it contains, and in the dynamic use of that space. The dome soars weightlessly overhead, seeming to float and billow like a gigantic hot-air balloon. Visitors stand in wonder within its vastness, at first reduced to insignificance and then absorbed into the cosmic illusion. The dome must have been so much more magnificent when girdled with Byzantine mosaics. But the day after the Turks took Constantinople, Hagia Sophia was converted to a mosque and in accordance with Islamic dogma all representational images had to be covered. Only in the 1930s, when Ataturk changed the church-cum-mosque into a museum, were the mosaics exposed once more. Those that could be saved were restored.

This is where **Doge Dandolo** was put to rest, in the southern gallery upstairs, but his sarcophagus has long been empty; his bones were removed by the Turks and thrown away.

Why it should be possible to put one's ear to the floor, listen to Dandolo's empty tomb and hear the trickle of water is not clear. There is nothing below the gallery floor other than vacant space filled by air. But it is true that below the narthex of his great church, Justinian built a vast cistern, nowadays called in Turkish the **Yerebatan Saray**, meaning the underground palace. Through much of the twentieth century, the cistern continued to serve its original purpose of storing the water brought to the city by the aqueduct of Valens. Its long avenues of 336 columns in 28 rows all have finely carved capitals; still in the same condition as when it was built, the cistern of today is exactly what our eyes would have seen had we lived in the sixth century.

This is where Bertrand Zobrist fixed his water-soluble sack of murky yellow-brown liquid, and beneath it, bolted to the floor, you may still see the polished titanium plaque that bears his inscription.

IN THIS PLACE, ON THIS DATE
THE WORLD WAS CHANGED FOREVER.

PART FOUR

DAN BROWN AND HIS WORLD

✳ CHAPTER TWELVE ✳

𝕷angdon & 𝕭rown

F lorence has long been familiar ground to Robert Langdon. At the end of *The Da Vinci Code* (2003), the second Langdon novel, after Sophie Neveu asks him when they can meet again, he tells her that he will be lecturing in Florence next month, where he will be given a room at the Hotel Brunelleschi. 'We'd be living in luxury', he suggests to her. 'You presume a lot, Mr Langdon', she replies, though she quickly accepts. On one condition: no museums, no churches, no art, no relics, no tombs, she insists. 'In Florence? For a week?' Langdon protests. 'There is nothing else to do!'

A LIFETIME KNOWLEDGE OF FLORENCE

In fact Langdon's familiarity with Florence goes back to his schooldays. In *The Lost Symbol* (2009), the third Langdon novel, he mentions Dante's *Inferno*, saying that nobody escaped Phillips Exeter Academy, an elite private school he attended in New Hampshire, without knowing the great Italian poet and the canticles of his *Divine Comedy*.

So at the beginning of the fourth Langdon novel, *Inferno*, when he regains consciousness at the hospital and sees the Palazzo Vecchio illuminated against the night sky, his surprise that he is somehow in Florence is nevertheless accompanied by phantasms and visions rooted in his long personal and cultural familiarity with the city, and especially with Dante's *Inferno*.

SYMBOLS AND QUESTS

But why does an otherwise laid-back Harvard University professor find himself in this succession of hair-raising adventures: in Rome; in Paris, London and Rosslyn; in Washington DC; and now in Florence, Venice and Istanbul? In each case he is summoned. He is wanted precisely because he is a world-renowned professor of religious symbology, whose specialities include classical iconology, symbols of pre-Christian culture, goddess art and the decryption of ancient ciphers. Also he is the author of more than a dozen books, including *The Symbology of Secret Sects*, *The Art of the Illuminati*, *The Lost Language of Ideograms*, *Symbols of the Lost Sacred Feminine* and the essential university textbook *Religious Iconology*.

If you are looking for answers in any of these areas – be it missing masonic treasures, the grotesque killings of a pope and cardinals, or the murder of a curator among the Leonardos at the Louvre – Robert Langdon is your man. And thus Robert Langdon finds himself in Florence once again, where there are riddles to be unravelled if the world is to be saved from the Shade and the vast but uncertain threat known only as Inferno.

To be summoned is one thing; to accept is another. And Langdon does have a remarkable history of getting himself involved in outrageous, dangerous and seemingly impossible challenges that would have defeated more ordinary men.

The questions they raise, and the demands they make on Langdon's physical and mental powers, amount less to a typical detective thriller case, and much more to something like a quest – in the mould of Homer's *Odyssey*, Virgil's *Aeneid*, Chrétien de Troyes' *Story of the Grail*, or for that matter Dante's *Inferno*.

A TOUCH OF CLAUSTROPHOBIA

While Langdon seemingly accepts his challenges with a ready ease, something as simple as being strapped into an aircraft seat fills him with dread. That happens at the start of *Angels and Demons* (2000), the very first of the Langdon books, when a hypersonic jet conveys him to Geneva. The cabin has all the appearance of a wide-bodied commercial airliner but it has no windows, 'which made Langdon uneasy'.

He has the same problem in Sienna Brooks' apartment in Florence early in *Inferno*. As he washes his wound and splashes water on his face, 'the windowless bathroom was suddenly feeling claustrophobic', and instinctively he steps into the hall towards a shaft of natural light. And later, while eluding his pursuers through the streets of Florence, the sight of the great red-tiled dome of the cathedral, the Duomo, reminds Langdon of an earlier visit to the city when 'he had foolishly decided to ascend the dome only to discover that its narrow, tourist crammed staircases were as distressing as any of the claustrophobic spaces he'd ever encountered'. That at least is understandable; there is even a sign at the entrance warning off visitors who feel uncomfortable in confined spaces. For Langdon, however, the feeling is extreme; it even follows him to London in *The Da Vinci Code*, where, entering the narrow low-ceilinged walkways in the grounds of Westminster Abbey,

Dan Brown with a man dressed as a Vatican Swiss Guard at the Rome premiere of the Angels and Demons *movie.*

he feels a touch of panic and considers how the word cloister is linked to the word claustrophobic.

Throughout his life Langdon has been haunted by 'a mild case of claustrophobia – the vestige of a childhood incident he had never quite overcome'. The condition has affected his life in many subtle ways: his aversion to indoor sports like squash, for example; foregoing inexpensive faculty housing and paying a small fortune to live in an airy, high-ceilinged Victorian home being another. Langdon even suspects that his attraction to the world of art as a young boy had much to do with his love of the vast spaces within museums.

THE BOOK OF THE DEAD

Langdon's fear of closed spaces becomes part of his ordeal, almost a necessary aspect of his quest. There is the terrifying scene in *The Lost Symbol* when the evil Mal'akh seals Langdon in a box and pumps it full of liquid. 'All he could do now was stare up through the blur of water above him and hope.' Unable to hold his breath any longer, 'His lips parted. His lungs expanded. And the liquid came pouring in. ... And then blackness. Robert Langdon was gone'. But not quite, it turns out, for this scene corresponds to the tenth hour of the Amduat, that part of the Egyptian *Book of the Dead* which deals with the soul's passage through the twelve hours of the night, when bodies of the deceased are suspended in the primeval waters of Nun. They appear to be drowning, but in fact they are being refreshed by the waters, and the promise is that they will be resurrected. 'O ye who whose cheeks are filled with water, whose souls have been deprived of their heavenly air, and who beat the air with your hands in order to obtain it, Come ye forth in this stream, for your members shall not perish, and your flesh shall not decay, and ye shall have dominion over the water, and your souls will have life.' It's not a spell that saves Langdon from drowning, however, but science. He has in fact been submerged in an oxygen-rich perfluorocarbon liquid – not something invented by Dan Brown, but a substance that is already finding medical uses. Whatever the means, Langdon has survived the ordeal and re-emerges, transformed and reborn as in the ancient myths, in

of it, even now, gives me a chill.' The young Dan remained on the ledge for some time, paralysed until help came. 'And then I got wrapped in a carpet.' As an adult, he does not like to talk about the incident, or even think about it. He lets Robert Langdon relive the fear for him. But like Langdon, ever since that terrible moment of what might have been, Dan Brown has seen the world in a different way, not quite so solid or reassuring as he had seen it before.

THE END DEPENDS UPON THE BEGINNING

Dan Brown admits that he created Robert Langdon as a fictional alter ego. 'Langdon's the guy I wish I could be.' Both Brown and Langdon were born on the same day in June; in the same town, Exeter, New Hampshire; and went to the same school, Phillips Exeter Academy, whose motto is 'The end depends upon the beginning'.

For all the similarities in their beginnings, their fears, and the success they have enjoyed in their respective careers, Dan

Brown's attempts at writing got off to an unpromising start. His first books were all flops; *Digital Fortress* (1998), *Angels and Demons* (2000) and *Deception Point* (2001) sold fewer than twenty thousand copies between them. One more book was due under Dan Brown's publishing contract; if that had failed too, he would have gone back to his quiet routine of teaching at his alma mater in Exeter. That things turned out differently was in large measure thanks to his wife Blythe, who guided him and was a driving force behind his success. Dan Brown's earliest inspiration, however, came from his hometown itself, from his schooling there and from his early family life.

PUZZLES AND GAMES

Dan Brown was born in Exeter, New Hampshire, on 22 June 1964, the son of a mathematics teacher at Phillips Exeter Academy and a mother he has described as 'a professional sacred musician'. He was raised as an Episcopalian. Both his parents sang in the church choir; his mother has a master's degree in sacred music and is a professional church organist.

Secrets and puzzles played a prominent role in Brown's childhood. His family had no television at home, and his parents' lives were saturated with mathematics and music. Those interests fused well, Brown says, with the family passion for anagrams, crossword puzzles and ciphers. On birthdays and at Christmas his father would create elaborate treasure hunts. Instead of finding their presents under the tree, Brown and his brother and sister would find treasure maps filled with codes and clues that would lead them from room to room throughout the house – or sometimes even around the town on their bicycles – sending them from one clue to the next until they finally discovered where their presents were hidden.

THE SACRED AND THE SECULAR

Aged five, Dan wrote his first book: *The Giraffe, the Pig and the Pants on Fire*. It came out as a limited one-copy homemade edition, which he still proudly owns. His sister is a painter, and his brother Gregory a musician. Gregory Brown has composed and performed the *Missa Charles Darwin*, which instead of a sacred text uses excepts from *On the Origin of Species*, *The Descent of Man*, and Darwin's correspondence.

That was one way to combine the religious and the rationalist strands in the Brown family; Dan, in his Robert Langdon novels, has found others. 'My mother was not at all shy about her Christianity', he says. The licence plate of his mother's red Volvo read KYRIE, meaning Lord in Greek, as in the chanted prayer Kyrie eleison, Lord have mercy. 'Her world was my reality, I believed in it.' But he also believed in his father's world of mathematics and science, and he enjoyed going out on summer nights and listening to his father talk about astronomy and about distant worlds and infinity. His father's white mini van bore a licence plate reading METRIC. Dan Brown was happy to live in those two worlds until the 'all-knowing age of thirteen'. That was the year he asked a priest which story was true, science or religion, to which he received the answer, 'Nice boys don't ask that question'.

Since the Renaissance and the time of Galileo, says Dan Brown, both science and religion have been vying for control of the truth. 'Religion wanted me to accept everything on faith which I found difficult, so I gravitated into science. But after a while the ground became mushy – relativity, uncertainty; matter does not exist, it is only a form of energy. But religious texts describe God as energy, and so the line between science and religion is starting to blur'.

FROM HERESY TO FLYING SAUCERS

Exeter, a New England town of barely 14,000 people, stands a few miles inland from the coast. It's located just up the Squamscott River, named after the Native American tribe from which the Reverend John Wheelwright bought the land in 1638. Wheelwright and 135 others were refugees from the Massachusetts Bay Colony, a Puritan theocracy; they were lucky to have been exiled and not hanged, for the charge against them was heresy. On 4 July the following year, they declared their settlement, named after Exeter in Devon, England, to be a self-governing and independent republic, and in 1775 it became the capital of revolutionary New Hampshire. The local Gilman family donated the first plot of land on which Phillips Exeter Academy now stands; they later contributed a Founding Father and a signatory of the United States Constitution, and one of their descendants now sits on the town's Board of Selectmen. An Exeter native, Daniel Chester French, sculpted the statue of Abraham Lincoln at the Lincoln Memorial in Washington, DC while the architect of the Memorial itself was Henry Bacon, who designed Exeter's Swasey Pavilion. The 'Exeter Incident', which took place the year after Dan Brown was born, was one of the most widely publicised and best documented of all UFO sightings. The little town of Exeter is a kind of microcosm of historical picturebook east-coast America.

PHILLIPS EXETER ACADEMY

Dan Brown is not the first best-selling writer in his family. His father, Richard G Brown, is the author of more than a dozen academic texts, including the best-selling *Advanced Mathematics: Precalculus with Discrete Mathematics and Data Analysis*, a standard work recommended at schools throughout the United States. Richard Brown has also received the Presidential Award for excellence in mathematics teaching.

Dan Brown and his siblings attended the school where their father taught. The wealthiest private school in the United States, Phillips Exeter Academy has the reputation of being the Eton of America. The roster of famous Exonians includes statesman Daniel Webster; Senator Jay Rockefeller; philanthropist David Rockefeller Jr; John Negroponte, former director of National Intelligence; novelist Gore Vidal; Peter Benchley, author of *Jaws*; novelist and critic James Agee; beer magnate Joseph Coors; chemicals baron and industrialist Pierre S du Pont; Drew Pearson, the 'yellow' journalist; historian Arthur Schlesinger Jr; President Franklin Pierce; Robert Lincoln, son of Abraham Lincoln; Ulysses S Grant Jr, son of Lincoln's general; and Mark Zuckerberg, founder of Facebook.

It may say something about Dan Brown's willingness to question the fundamental assumptions of our society that Phillips Exeter is renowned for using the Harkness method of teaching and has a student-teacher ratio of five to one. Every course at Exeter, whether calculus, literature or existential philosophy, is taught around an oval table, with the idea that learning should come as much from the interchange between students as from the teacher. The school seal, as pictured on p.228, is Masonic in its imagery, and depicts a river, the sun and a beehive.

After finishing at Phillips Exeter, Dan Brown attended Amherst, a venerable Massachusetts liberal arts college, where he took a double major in English and Spanish and showed an interest in music composition and creative writing. He spent his junior year studying the history of art at the University of Seville, and graduated from Amherst in 1986. He would later put his experience of Seville to use when writing his first novel, *Digital Fortress*.

THE MYSTERIOUS BLYTHE NEWLON

There's much more to the Dan Brown story, however, than simply looking for parallels between the author and his hero, Robert Langdon. Another element plays a part in the creation of the Langdon novels – in the themes certainly, and possibly in the character of Langdon himself, giving him a certain small-boy sense of secrecy and vulnerability that makes him both sympathetic and attractive to women. This element is Mrs Dan Brown.

The dedication in *Inferno* is 'For my parents', and frankly it's about time too. Because the dedication in *Angels and Demons* reads, 'For Blythe'. In *The Da Vinci Code* it reads, 'For Blythe ... again. More than ever.' And in *The Lost Symbol* it once more reads simply, 'For Blythe'. 'My wife has always been a tremendous support system,' as Dan Brown puts it.

Dan Brown with Blythe Newlon and Renaud Donnedieu de Vabres, the French culture minister, at the 2006 Cannes Film Festival.

Mrs Dan Brown was born Blythe Newlon in Palmdale, a high desert town in Los Angeles County, California, in about 1952. That would make her twelve years older than her husband. Both the date and place of birth are uncertain, because almost everything about her is veiled in secrecy – in which role Dan Brown may have introduced her into the first chapter of his *Inferno* as the woman who appears to Langdon in a vision and tells him time is short, seek and find. 'The woman reached up and slowly lifted the veil from her face. She was strikingly beautiful, and yet older than Langdon had imagined – in her 60s perhaps, stately and strong, like a timeless statue ... Langdon sensed he knew her ... trusted her. But how? Why?'

Blythe does not give interviews. Nor has she made public even the barest outlines of her life before 1991, when, as the influential director of artistic development at the National Academy For Songwriters in Los Angeles, she first met Dan Brown. Clutching a portfolio of his songs and a demo CD, he was hoping to hit the big time as a singer-composer.

Brown admits he was a curious sight, describing himself as 'a fish out of water in Los Angeles'. Teaching Spanish at Beverly Hills Preparatory School by day, and chasing a career in music by night, he lived in a low-rent apartment complex whose hallways overflowed with male models, stand-up comics, aspiring rock stars and drama queens. Blythe, in her late-thirties, was an attractive woman with an established career, and within no time was making things happen.

She took the unusual step for an Academy executive of becoming Brown's manager, and promoted his debut CD with an announcement to the trade that 'we fully expect Dan Brown will some day be included in the ranks of our [the Academy's] most successful members, talents like Billy Joel, Paul Simon and Prince'. Secretly they became lovers. Stardom failed to call, however, and eventually Dan Brown concluded that 'the world isn't ready for a pale, balding geek shaking his booty; it's not a pretty picture'. Meanwhile, though, he and Blythe took a holiday to Tahiti in 1993, and he came across an old copy of Sidney Sheldon's *The Doomsday Conspiracy* on the beach: 'I read the first page ... and then the next ... and then the next. Several hours later, I finished the book and thought, "Hey, I can do that."'

A few months later, Brown took Blythe home to genteel Exeter, where he got a job teaching at Phillips Exeter Academy and in his spare time, with Blythe's enthusiastic support, began to write. They married in 1997.

THE BIG IDEA

Brown's childhood love of puzzles, codes and treasure hunts easily transitioned as he grew older into the creation of a fictional world where the hero undertakes a quest through a landscape of secret organisations and hidden truths. All his books deal with secrecy in one way or another, whether in the guise of spy agencies, conspiracy theories, classified technologies or – and this was Dan Brown's biggest discovery – secret history.

Each time he has approached a new novel, Dan Brown has looked for what he calls the 'big idea'. And big for Dan Brown gets bigger all the time, reaching out to a cosmic scale. The ideas are preposterous: in *Angels and Demons*, the Illuminati return after two centuries to destroy the Vatican using anti-matter; in *The Da Vinci Code*, Jesus and Mary Magdalene establish a church based on the worship of the sacred feminine, their bloodline continuing down to the present day; and in *The Lost Symbol*, our entire civilisation is called into question over the separation of faith from science since the Renaissance – a denial of the divine potential of mankind.

Not many writers would have the sheer gall to take on subjects of that scale, and neither could anyone expect that the Nicene Creed or Hermes Trismegistus or Thomas Malthus would become the stuff of thrillers read by millions of people around the world. Yet Dan Brown has a gift for making the outrageous and arcane seem natural and accessible. Part of the explanation lies in the sheer pace of his adventures, the short cliff-hanging chapters driving the reader on.

On top of that, though, Dan Brown seems to share the deep-seated doubts and half-realised thoughts of the public mind, often on the most serious and daunting of matters, and he is able to form them into compelling and enjoyable stories. 'I think my books contain a lot of meat', he says, 'but it tastes like dessert somehow.'

DISCOVERING ROBERT LANGDON

Angels and Demons (2000) was the first Robert Langdon novel, *The Da Vinci Code* (2003) was the second, *The Lost Symbol* (2009) was the third, and now *Inferno* (2013) is the fourth. 'It was a real joy for me to write,' Brown has said of *Angels and Demons*, 'and a breakthrough in terms of finding my own style, although I can only say that with hindsight'. He went on:

> I intend to make Robert Langdon my primary
> character for years to come. His expertise in
> symbology and iconography affords him the luxury
> of potentially limitless adventures in exotic locales.
> It was also a book in which Blythe could be more
> involved, as she has a great love of art and art history.

That last remark, about Blythe becoming involved, gives a clue to the entire development of the Robert Langdon novels, both their themes and the character of Langdon himself.

Brown worried that his first book, *Digital Fortress*, with its theme of privacy and surveillance in the new computer era, was too overtly a techno-thriller. With *Angels and Demons* he changed direction towards conspiracy and art, and this is where Robert Langdon made his debut. Together with Vittoria Vetra, a sensuous and beautiful woman scientist, Langdon attempts to find a canister of anti-matter stolen from CERN, the European Organisation for Nuclear Research. A message from the Illuminati, a deeply anti-Christian secret society, says the canister is hidden somewhere in the Vatican where its explosive power can blow the holy city to kingdom come. Also gone missing are the preferiti, the four cardinals shortlisted to succeed the recently deceased pope.

Propelled through the Vatican and round the Renaissance monuments of Bernini in Rome by a series of clues, and assisted by the Camerlengo, the late pope's closest aide, Langdon and Vittoria search for the cardinals in the hope that they will find the stolen anti-matter. Instead they discover that each of the preferiti has been murdered in a peculiarly symbolic and gruesome way. When Langdon finds the first, his mouth stuffed with earth, he recognises this as a further message from the Illuminati: Earth, Air, Fire, Water are the ancient elements from which all the world is made, meaning that three more victims are intended. Meanwhile a digital clock linked to the anti-matter canister continues its twenty-four hour countdown to Armageddon.

Dan Brown took a wrong turn with *Deception Point*, a boys'-toys thriller focusing on the intelligence activities of America's National Reconnaissance Office, which despite having a $10 billion budget and more than 10,000 employees, is unknown to most American taxpayers. One can immediately see how Robert Langdon would have been out of place among its stealth ships and secret aircraft heading for the North Pole.

THE GREAT HIDDEN SECRET

Next, however, Brown had the idea of using a novel to ask 'what it would mean for Christianity if Jesus were more like us, not God but man?' The result was *The Da Vinci Code*. 'My hope in writing this novel', he said, 'was that the story would serve as a catalyst and a springboard for people to discuss the important topics of faith, religion and history.' With its premise of a great secret hidden within the code – that Jesus was married to Mary Magdalene and, after his crucifixion, she escaped to France where she gave birth to their child and propagated his bloodline which survives to this day – he touched off a firestorm that swept around the globe. *The Da Vinci Code* became the world's best-selling adult novel. Its appeal is three-fold: it's a top-grade page-turner of a thriller, it packs in more conspiracy per page than almost any other novel you can name, and it has

a backdrop of religion, art and secrecy that somehow hits a vein in our supposedly secular modern world.

Dan Brown had researched the material for *Digital Fortress* and *Deception Point* entirely on his own, but his wife Blythe became what he has called his 'research assistant' on the Robert Langdon novels *Angels and Demons* and *The Da Vinci*

As book and film, The Da Vinci Code *conquered the world – here Tom Hanks and Audrey Tautou get set for Korea.*

Code. 'This was wonderful', he said. 'We were able to work together as husband and wife.' Blythe did much of the research into some of the most colourful and intriguing themes in *The Da Vinci Code*, and she was at the very least an indispensable creative force. It was Blythe who suggested her husband introduce the bloodline theory to the book, combining it with suppressed goddess worship and the idea of a Church of Magdalene that never was. At first he was reluctant, he has openly admitted; he thought the idea was too incredible, 'a step too far'. But eventually she convinced him:

> *Blythe's female perspective was particularly helpful with* The Da Vinci Code, *which deals so heavily with concepts like the sacred feminine, goddess worship and the feminine aspect of spirituality. I'm not sure I had ever seen Blythe as passionate about anything as she became for the historical figure of Mary Magdalene, particularly the idea that the Church had unfairly maligned her.*

ANCIENT MYSTERIES AND MODERN SCIENCE

The partnership continued a few years later with *The Lost Symbol*, a book that can also be described as the combined effort of Dan and Blythe Brown. 'Blythe is helping me with the research for my new novel', he said. 'Our studies into the origins of the Christian movement and the ancient mysteries continue to this day.'

Noetic science, intention experiments and the Ancient Mysteries all sound like subjects that Blythe could have drawn her husband into, and on which they would have worked happily together, sharing their interests. Indeed, it is interesting to note how close the sceptical Robert Langdon is drawn to the ideas of Katherine Solomon at the end of the novel, she the older woman, the harbinger of a new way of looking at the world, who sees faith and science as a whole and realises the divinity of mankind.

INTO THE INFERNO

'This is the darkest novel yet', Dan Brown says of his Inferno. 'I want to stress that this is not an activist book. But overpopulation is something that I'm concerned about.' Which raises the question of whether the world really is overpopulated, and whether the current rate of population increase will continue for much longer – issues that are considered in Chapter Eight of this book. Dan Brown, at any rate, believes so. Taking Dante's Inferno, with its grotesque images of the human condition, as his launchpad, he explores the scientific and moral issues involved in a new 'plague' being unleashed by the scientific genius Bertrand Zobrist, who believes that the only way to save the world from the consequences of rampant overpopulation is to wipe out a large proportion of the human race.

✳ CHAPTER THIRTEEN ✳

An Infernal Glossary

Pretty women, lanky men, bearded doctors, handsome academics, exhaling editors, doomsayer lunatics, silver-haired devils and chthonic monsters: Dan Brown's *Inferno* runs the gamut of human, posthuman and Transhuman types. Here's a who's who and who's not who to the book's characters, from Dante Alighieri to Bertrand Zobrist, along with some of the concepts, fabrics and organisations that may have left you bemused as to the Dan Brown web of fact and fiction.

ALIGHIERI, DANTE The author of the *Divine Comedy* (1265–1321), and the inspiration for Dan Brown's *Inferno*; see Chapter One for the full story of Dante's life.

ALVAREZ, MARTA The petite and pregnant arts and culture administrator who shows Robert Langdon around the Palazzo Vecchio. She is based on a real person as in the book's acknowledgements Dan Brown thanks 'the bright Marta Alvarez González' for spending so much time with us in Florence.

ANTONUCCI, EUGENIA A secretary at the Museo dell'Opera del Duomo, Eugenia is distressed to hear of the death of her boss, the corpulent Ignazio Busoni: 'the woman was weeping now, her voice full of sadness'. Dan Brown thanks a real-life Eugenia Antonucci for her help at the Bibliotecca Medicea Laurenziana.

ARCA Some years before the events depicted in *Inferno*, Robert Langdon saw a display by the prominent equine theatrical troupe Behind The Mask in New Hampshire. He so admired their jet-black Friesian mounts that he researched the breed online. Finding that such animals had inspired the robust aesthetic of the Horses of St Mark's, and that said equestrian statues had repeatedly been stolen, he visited the website of the Association for Research into Crimes against Art, to learn more. The Association does exist, www.artcrimeresearch.org

ATELIER PIETRO LONGHI As Dan Brown so rightly says, the Atelier Pietro Longhi is one of Venice's premier providers of historical costumes.

BOTTICELLI, SANDRO The life and work of Sandro Botticelli (c. 1445–1510), considered by Robert Langdon among others to be 'one of the true giants of the Renaissance', is examined in Chapter Six. His *Map of Hell* is a central image in Dan Brown's *Inferno*, and is reproduced on pp.148–149 of this book.

BROOKS, SIENNA At the age of five the fictional character Sienna Brooks played the mischievous Puck in *A Midsummer Night's Dream* at the London Globe Theatre (renamed the Gielgud Theatre in 1994 and not to be confused with the modern recreation of Shakespeare's Globe); she is no less an actress in adulthood. But there is nothing put on about

The Behind The Mask equine troupe, as seen by Robert Langdon – or was it Dan Brown? – at a celebrity wedding reception in New Hampshire.

her need to wear a blonde wig; her hair loss is the result of a stress-related scalp disorder which she describes as 'telegenic effluvium' – probably a slip of the tongue for the condition 'telogen effluvium' – which was triggered by a traumatic event that led her to train as a doctor and to devote her life to saving the world.

BRÜDER, CRISTOPH Another fictional character, this former military man with an umlaut over his name and an emotionless sense of duty works in the Surveillance and Response Support division of the European Centre for Disease Prevention and Control. He operates under the authority of Elizabeth Sinskey, director of the World Health Organisation.

BRUNELLESCHI, FILIPPO As explained in Chapter Five, Filippo Brunelleschi (1377–1446) was a pivotal figure in the emergence of humanism in Florence. He was responsible for constructing the dome that tops the city's Santa Maria del Fiore cathedral, and as Dan Brown describes, his sculpted figure can still be seen 'seated outside the Palazzo dei Canonici, staring contentedly up at his masterpiece'.

BUSONI, IGNAZIO The fictional director of the Museo dell'Opera del Duomo, that is the Museum of Works of the Cathedral in Florence, containing works of art originally intended for Santa Maria del Fiore. He is popularly known as il Duomino, translated as 'little dome' in the book, though, more exactly, *duomo* means cathedral (from the Latin *domus*, house, as in house of God); therefore *il Duomino* would mean 'little cathedral'. At any rate he is an oversized man in every way.

COLLINS This is the name of the man who introduces himself over the phone to Robert Langdon as the American Consul General's chief administrator in Florence, a reminder that you should believe only half of what you see and nothing of what you hear.

CONSORTIUM, THE Dan Brown announces in the 'Fact' section at the start of *Inferno* that 'The Consortium is a private organisation with offices in seven countries. Its name has been changed for considerations of security and privacy.' In interviews to promote the book, he elaborated: 'The Consortium is obviously not the real name. There are a number of organisations that function as the Consortium. They are fairly easy to research. I had not heard of them until I started writing this novel. But they're out there and for hire and allow you to tell very convincing lies.' At one point in *Inferno*, the provost reflects that the experience with Bertrand Zobrist 'would not be the first time the Consortium had been hired by paranoid scientists and engineers who preferred working in extreme isolation'.

COUNCIL ON FOREIGN RELATIONS A non-profit American thinktank, the Council on Foreign Relations was founded in 1921, and does indeed have its headquarters at Park and 68th in New York. It's not clear, however, why Bertrand Zobrist has access to its conference rooms.

DANDOLO, ENRICO The 'wizened, blind doge' of Venice, Enrico Dandolo (c. 1107–1205) was well into his nineties when he led the conquest of Constantinople in 1204, and died there the following year. Robert Langdon's realisation that Dandolo is not buried in Venice and that he must head to the doge's tomb in Istanbul – 'Sienna, we're in the wrong country' – is a startling moment in Dan Brown's *Inferno*, not only for its drama, but because any student of Venetian or Byzantine history and art, let alone a Harvard professor, should have known that.

DANIKOVA The panicked woman with a thick Eastern European accent who blurts out helpful if highly sensitive information on Sienna's answering machine. It may be her poor grasp of English that leads her to imagine that as a British national Sienna would require a working visa in Italy; citizens of member states of the European Union are, in fact, free to travel, live and work anywhere within the EU without a visa.

DOOMSDAY CLOCK In chapter 50 of *Inferno*, Bertrand Zobrist is credited with having created a Doomsday Clock, which shows that 'if the entire span of human life on earth were compressed into a single hour ... we are now in its final seconds'. Although Bertrand's clock takes population as its reference point, the actual Doomsday Clock has been maintained since 1947 by the *Bulletin of the Atomic Scientists*. Rather than ticking steadily down, it's adjusted back and forth according to their perception of the threat of nuclear catastrophe.

ERNST, MAX In chapter 2 of *Inferno*, Robert Langdon feels as though he has awoken inside a painting by the German-born Max Ernst (1891–1976), a pioneer of the Dada movement and surrealism who lived in France and the United States. Dan Brown does not specify which painting he felt he had woken up in, but Ernst did write a memoir that was modelled on Dante's *Vita Nuova*. It featured his alter ego, the Bird Superior Loplop, which he also painted many times.

ESCHER, M C As mentioned in chapter 72 of *Inferno*, M C Escher (1898–1972) was a brilliant graphic artist whose birthplace, the Dutch province of Friesland, gave its name to the kind of large-bodied horse that served as the model for the Horses of St Mark's in Venice.

ESFANDIARY, FEREIDOUN M The handsome Iranian man described in chapter 73 of *Inferno*, F M Esfandiary (1930–2000) was indeed an early prophet of Transhumanism who changed his name to FM-2030 in the hope that he would celebrate his 100th birthday in 2030.

FM-2030

EUROPEAN CENTRE FOR DISEASE PREVENTION AND CONTROL Based in Stockholm, the ECDC 'works in partnership with national health protection bodies across Europe to strengthen and develop continent-wide disease surveillance and early warning systems'. It does have a Surveillance and Response Support section, but there's no record of it using miniature drone helicopters to shoot indiscriminately through museum windows.

FAUKMAN, JONAS Robert Langdon's New York-based editor. The name is a deft anagram of Dan Brown's real-life 'editor and close friend Jason Kaufman'.

FERRIS, JONATHAN A fictional character wearing Plume Paris glasses in Dan Brown's *Inferno*, Ferris apparently works for the World Health Organisation. But nothing is as simple as that.

GULENSOY, GOKSEL The Turkish documentary filmmaker mentioned in chapter 84 of *Inferno* has devoted twenty years to filming the tunnels and cisterns under Hagia Sophia. Take a look at www.beneaththehagiasophia.com to see images, and read how delighted he is to find that his work has been mentioned by Dan Brown.

GYPSY, THE Years of carrying her wares around St Mark's Square in Venice have given the Gypsy strong arms that she puts to profitable use when, after some bargaining over the price, she agrees to haul a dark-haired man and a pretty young woman out of a narrow light well beneath the piazza.

HARRIS TWEED A handwoven cloth from the Outer Hebrides, used to make the kind of well-tailored jackets favoured by Robert Langdon.

HIRST, DAMIEN Like Robert Langdon, Dan Brown saw British artist Damien Hirst's diamond-encrusted skull, *For The Love Of God*, on display in the Palazzo Vecchio. Interviewed by *Time* magazine, Brown commented 'I love the blend of the old and new, and Damien Hirst does that beautifully'. He also said that he'd be flattered to be spoken of in the same breath as Hirst.

KENNEDY, JOHN F As Dan Brown acknowledges in chapter 38 of *Inferno*, the epigraph for his book – 'the darkest places in hell are reserved for those who maintain their neutrality in times of moral crisis' – is not a genuine quotation from the *Divine Comedy*. It's merely 'derived from the work of Dante', and, as explained on p.21, it does not accurately Dante's depiction of Hell. It comes in fact from a speech delivered by President John F Kennedy (1917–63) in Germany, in June 1963: 'Dante once said that the hottest places in hell are reserved for those who in a period of moral crisis maintain their neutrality'.

KEYMEL, MARIELE The real and world-renowned pianist is described in *Inferno* as having given a spectacular concert of classical music in the Hall of the Five Hundred. True; during a year spent studying in Florence, Mariele Keymel (1951–2011) took part in a performance of Beethoven's complete piano sonatas in the Palazzo Vecchio.

KIER, DEB This character appears in the pages of *Inferno* as an owner services representative with NetJets, based in Columbus, Ohio. The company is real, with operations in North America, Europe and China, but it is not clear if Deb Kier is a real person or not.

KLIMT, GUSTAV Seeing *The Kiss*, by the Viennese Symbolist painter Gustav Klimt (1862–1918), displayed in Venice's Ca'

Pesaro, was responsible for arousing the American symbologist Robert Langdon's lifelong gusto for modern art. Though Langdon does not say so, the theme of a couple embraced in a kiss associates the painting with Rodin's sculpture, *The Kiss*, which was inspired by the characters of Paolo and Francesca in Dante's *Inferno*.

KNOWLTON, LAURENCE Described in Dan Brown's *Inferno* as a senior facilitator for the Consortium aboard its headquarters yacht the Mendacium, Knowlton is a fictional character whose task is to release Zobrist's video to the world, but alarm bells go off when he previews it.

KURZWEIL, RAY Credited with developing the first OCR – optical character recognition – software in the 1970s, Ray Kurzweil is a real person who is also a leading advocate of Transhumanism in general, and especially, as described in

Chapter Thirteen of this book, of the idea that humanity is approaching the 'Singularity', the sudden and irreversible moment in which artificial intelligence exceeds human brain power for the first time. As of 2013, he's director of engineering at Google, tasked with transforming the Google search engine into a 'cybernetic friend'.

Ray Kurzweil – the man at the heart of actual Transhumanism.

LANGDON, ROBERT A Harvard professor of religious iconology and symbology, Langdon is the fictional hero of four Dan Brown novels. Even when being shot at and chased round Florence he finds the time to describe paintings, churches and the like, though perhaps because of a childhood mishap, when he fell down a well, his descriptions are not always accurate.

LONGFELLOW, HENRY WADSWORTH As described in chapter

18 of *Inferno*, New England's famous Fireside Poet (1807–82) published the first American translation of Dante's *Divine Comedy* in 1867, and founded the Dante Society of America the year before his death. In Matthew Pearl's 2003 novel, *The Dante Club*, Longfellow and his fellow poets use their Dantean expertise to unmask a serial killer.

Fireside Poet and translator of Dante, Henry Wadsworth Longfellow.

MACHIAVELLI, NICCOLÓ The Fiorentine politician whose name is a byword for double-dealing, Niccoló Machiavelli (1469–1527) wrote his most famous work, *The Prince*, after being removed from power by the Medici. The quotation cited by Elizabeth Sinskey in chapter 22 of *Inferno* comes from his *Discourses on Livy*, and reads in full: 'When every province of the world so teems with inhabitants that they can neither subsist where they are nor remove themselves elsewhere, every region being equally crowded and over-peopled, and when human craft and wickedness have reached their highest peak, it must needs come about that the world will purge itself in one or another of these three ways, to the end that men, becoming few and contrite, may amend their lives and live with more convenience.' The three ways in question are very much the Malthusian checks described in Chapter Seven of this book: floods, plagues and famines.

MALTHUS, THOMAS ROBERT The life and work of Thomas Robert Malthus (1766–1834) forms the subject of Chapter Seven of this book.

MARCONI, ENRICO The doctor who appears at the beginning of *Inferno* where he is working with Dr Sienna Brooks in the hospital where Robert Langdon regains consciousness. He is fictional in more ways than one.

MCKENNITT, LOREENA One of Robert Langdon's favourite living recording artists, the Canadian harpist, accordionist and pianist Loreena McKennitt, mentioned in chapter 15 of *Inferno*, wrote a song called 'Dante's Prayer'. A karaoke version is available on *Karaoke Pop Hits volume 69*.

MENDACIUM, THE A key component of the Consortium's ingenious strategy to remain inconspicuous, the Mendacium is a gigantic yacht, owned by a man known as the provost, which sails around the Mediterranean looking like a futuristic warship. Nor does its name give anything away, unless you realise that *mendacium* comes from the Latin for lie or fiction.

MIRSAT The fictional curator of the Hagia Sophia, the sixth-century church–mosque–museum in Istanbul, which he specially opens after hours for Langdon in his search for the doomsday device.

OPPENHEIMER, J. ROBERT In chapter 15 of *Inferno*, Sienna Brooks quotes J. Robert Oppenheimer (1904–67), the 'Father of the Atomic Bomb', as saying 'I am Vishnu, destroyer of worlds' when he witnessed the first A-bomb test on July 16

Professor J. Robert Oppenheimer (right) with General Leslie Groves, military head of the Manhattan Project, which developed the Atomic Bomb.

1945. The correct quotation, from the *Bhagavad Gita*, is 'Now I am become Death, the destroyer of worlds', and Oppenheimer himself later wrote that he only *remembered* the words, he didn't actually *say* them.

PIMPONI, MAURIZIO The skipper of the boat in which Langdon, Sienna and Ferris zip along the Grand Canal in Venice, his character is perhaps based on the 'peerless' Maurizio Pimponi credited by Dan Brown in his acknowledgements.

POPULATION APOCALYPSE EQUATION In chapter 41 of *Inferno*, Sienna Brooks describes Bertrand Zobrist as a proponent of the Population Apocalypse Equation, which is said to be a mathematical recognition that thanks to overpopulation we are facing the apocalyptic collapse of society. There is no such equation. Search for it online, however, and you'll find all sorts of conspiracy theorists who allege that President Obama's director for counterterrorism wrote a master's thesis on the Apocalypse Equation, which argued that the US government should instigate a 'planned and controlled genocide' in the face of declining fossil fuel reserves. There's no evidence that such a thesis exists either. Pacifist Bradford Lyttle published an Apocalypse Equation in the 1980s, but that, like the Doomsday Clock, centred on the possibility of nuclear war or conflagration.

PLUME PARIS The European-influenced brand of glasses worn by Jonathan Ferris. As the Florida-based company's website makes clear, the glasses are available in 22 different styles, in order to satisfy whatever the wearer has in mind, and, significantly, feature unique temple designs. Some are made out of Zyl to achieve beautiful colours, while others are made with Stainless Steel Metal.

PORTINARI, BEATRICE For the full story of Beatrice Portinari (1266–90), the great idealised love of Dante's life, see Chapter Two. As Dan Brown describes, her 'simple sepulchre has become a pilgrimage destination for both Dante fans and heartsick lovers alike'.

PROVOST, THE Head of the Consortium and owner of the yacht Mendacium, he offers invisibility to anyone with the money.

RODIN, AUGUSTE The French sculptor Auguste Rodin (1840–1917) is mentioned in chapter 15 of *Inferno* as having created the sculpture *The Three Shades*. It's an interesting story. Rodin did a monumental sculpture of the *Gates of Hell*, whose 186 figures were inspired by Dante's *Inferno*. The figures later emerged as separate sculptures, among them *The Three Shades*, *The Thinker* and his famous *The Kiss*. See pages 70–71 of this book for more about *The Kiss*.

RUSSO, ERNESTO The Pitti Palace security guard who is treated to an example of Sienna Brooks' mastery of *dim mak*.

SERACINI, MAURIZIO The now-famous art diagnostician who spotted Vasari's hidden message on the *Battle of Marciano* in the Palazzo Veccio – 'Cerca Trova' – Maurizio Seracini crops up twice in *Inferno*, and also figured in *The Da Vinci Code*.

SHADE, THE Dan Brown's *Inferno* opens with a mysterious figure who calls himself the Shade running through the pre-dawn streets of Florence. To escape capture he leaps from the spire of the Badia, leaving behind what he calls his gift to mankind, otherwise known as Inferno. After a number of twists and turns and clues, the Shade turns out to be ... but you will have to read the book.

The French sculptor Auguste Rodin photographed in 1893.

SINSKEY, ELIZABETH The World Health Organisation is real, but the character of Elizabeth Sinskey, its director in Dan Brown's novel, is fiction. But there are fictions within fictions in *Inferno*, and it takes some time for the reader to appreciate the truth about Sinskey, and for her to discover the truth about herself.

SOLUBLON A widely used water soluble material manufactured by Japan's Aicello Chemical Company, Solublon has many applications, include packaging laundry detergent and printing transfers. According to Aicello's website, if you have an idea for a new use – infecting the planet with a latter-day version of the Black Death by suspending it in a Byzantine cistern, for example – 'we can help craft the concept into a genuine product'.

VASARI, GIORGIO Painter, architect and art historian, Giorgio Vasari (1511–74) built and decorated many of the sites in Dan Brown's Inferno, from the Vasari Corridor to various chambers in the Palazzo Vecchio to the fresco in the dome of the Duomo. A student of Michelangelo and a favourite of the Medicis, he knew everyone who was anyone in mid-sixteenth century Florence; in his *Lives of the Artists* he describes Botticelli's obsession with Dante, which led, as Dan Brown writes in chapter 18 of *Inferno*, to 'serious disorders in his living'.

VAYENTHA When the fictional Vayentha dismounts from her BMW motorbike and bursts into the hospital where Langdon is regaining consciousness and opens fire, the great chase begins. In fact there might have been no Dan Brown novel at all had she finished the job the day before, as intended, but she was disturbed by the cooing of a dove.

VENCI, GIORGIO Something of a *deus ex machina*, the possibly fictional chief designer of the real Atelier Pietro Longhi is a Wizard of Oz figure who prefers to work his magic from behind a curtain and gives Sienna a helping hand when all seems lost.

VIO, ETTORE The jovial-looking white-haired curator of the Basilica of St Mark in Venice, who's delighted to drop every-thing and tease Robert Langdon with cryptic clues as to the identity of Enrico Dandolo. In real life, Ettore Vio has indeed

Giorgio Vasari, author of Lives of the Artists.

written books about St Mark's, so it's presumably a slip of the keyboard when Dan Brown acknowledges the help of 'Ettore Vito'.

WORLD HEALTH ORGANISATION The public health agency of the United Nations primarily concerns itself with the eradication of existing diseases like smallpox, malaria and TB, and the threat posed by new ones such as HIV/AIDS and variants of bird flu. Its current director general, Dr Margaret Chan, is on record as saying 'Access to modern contraception is a fundamental right of every woman'.

ZOBRIST, BERTRAND The fictional geneticist and Swiss billionaire Bertrand Zobrist is a Transhumanist, has developed a new line in viruses, and is a Dante enthusiast. Just the sort of fellow Dan Brown might write a book about.

❋ CHAPTER FOURTEEN ❋

𝕱urther 𝕽eading and 𝖂ebsites

WORKS BY DANTE ALIGHIERI

Depending on the reader's preference, in particular as to whether to read Dante in prose or verse, the following versions are recommended. They are clear and readable, and are also highly accurate translations.

THE DIVINE COMEDY by Dante Alighieri
Translated by John D Sinclair, OUP 1961.
Italian text with English prose translation and commentary in three volumes.

THE DIVINE COMEDY by Dante Alighieri
Verse translation by C H Sisson, Oxford World's Classics 1993.
The pick of modern verse translations.

VITA NUOVA by Dante Alighieri
Translated by Mark Musa, Oxford World's Classics 1992.
In the *Vita Nuova*, the 'New Life', Dante tells the story of his own youthful development as a poet, and of his love for Beatrice. Written in prose and poetry before he began the *Divine Comedy*, it has been called a psychobiography for the insights it offers into Dante's mind.

BIOGRAPHY

LIFE OF DANTE by Giovanni Boccaccio
Translated by Philip H Wicksteed, Oneworld Classics 2009.
The earliest authority we have for events in Dante's life, apart from Dante himself, is his first biographer, Giovanni Boccaccio, whose researches included talking with people still alive who had first-hand memories of the poet. Boccaccio, the author of the *Decameron*, was one of the great writers of the Renaissance, and his brief life of Dante is a delight to read.

DANTE'S INVENTION by James Burge
The History Press 2010.
As well as being a writer, Burge directs and produces films for television, and in his excellent life of Dante he naturally responds to Dante's visual imagination. That he does so with the freshness of someone who may be encountering Dante for the first time makes his book easy and enjoyable to read, while not lacking in authority.

DANTE IN LOVE by A N Wilson
Atlantic Books 2011.
Oddly, English author A N Wilson complained in a review of Dan Brown's *Inferno* that it had obviously been written with the making of the film in mind. That is exactly how Dante himself reads, however, and especially his *Inferno*, the modern appeal of which very much depends on Dante's powerful and often perversely funny talent for imagery. A lifelong Dante enthusiast, Wilson observes in this superb study how the self-proclaimed poet of love could also be the poet of hate, vengeance, implacable resentment and everlasting feuds, who dispatched personal enemies to the inferno to be mired in their own excrement, or forever be eaten by their demented neighbours.

ESOTERISM

What with his Beatrice and his numerology, and lines in the *Inferno* such as 'O, you possessed of sturdy intellect, observe the teachings hidden here, beneath the veil of verses so obscure', Dante has long served as a magnet for every kind of fantastical interpretation about what he really means.

THE CRYPTOGRAPHY OF DANTE by Walter Arensberg
Alfred Knopf 1921.

Arensberg, a wealthy American art collector and critic, also an English literature graduate of Harvard, sees Dante's *Inferno* as a journey inside his mother, full of sexual symbolism; Beatrice, he maintains, was really Bella, Dante's mum, a conclusion he supports by deciphering the many cryptograms he has found in Dante's works.

THE ESOTERISM OF DANTE by René Guénon
Sophia Perennis 1996.

A French metaphysical writer of the early twentieth century, also known as Shaykh Abd al-Wahid Yahya, Guénon maintains that Dante must be understood on four levels of meaning: the literal, the philosophical, the political and the initiatic. The last touches on hermeticism, the Templars, Rosicrucianism, the Freemasons and extra-terrestrial journeys.

THE BLACK DEATH

THE DECAMERON by Giovanni Boccaccio
Available in numerous editions.

The best account ever written of the Black Death. Dante's biographer Giovanni Boccaccio prefaces the tales of his *Decameron* with his eyewitness record of the plague's devastating effects in Florence.

ONLINE SOURCES FOR DANTE

The following online sources provide a wealth of easily accessible material about Dante and his world, including his works in the original Italian and various English translations.

PRINCETON DANTE PROJECT
etcweb.princeton.edu/dante

DIGITAL DANTE AT COLUMBIA UNIVERSITY
dante.ilt.columbia.edu

THE WORLD OF DANTE
www.worldofdante.org

BOTTICELLI

SANDRO BOTTICELLI: THE DRAWINGS FOR DANTE'S DIVINE COMEDY
Royal Academy of Arts 2000.

The mystery, grace and sensuality of Renaissance art achieves its zenith in such works as the *Birth of Venus* and *Primavera* by Sandro Botticelli. In the drawings he did for Dante's *Divine Comedy* you recognise the form and features of Venus in Beatrice, but this is a very different world; Botticelli had become an avid supporter of the fanatical religious theocrat Savonarola. Botticelli's *Map of Hell*, one of the drawings in this series, was probably done around the time that he witnessed the hanging and burning of Savonarola for heresy in Florence.

POPULATION ISSUES

FEEDING FRENZY by Paul McMahon
Profile Books 2013.

Chapter Eight of *Inferno Decoded* is a condensed version of one chapter of this authoritative study of 'The New Politics Of Food'. In the rest of *Feeding Frenzy*, McMahon outlines the steps that need to be taken to shape a sustainable and just global food system.

AN ESSAY ON THE PRINCIPLES OF POPULATION by Thomas Robert Malthus
Oxford World's Classics.

Whether or not you have any sympathy for his ideas, it's worth reading Malthus's original 1798 essay, in which they're expressed with the utmost clarity.

TRANSHUMANISM AND THE FUTURE OF SCIENCE

AN OPTIMIST'S TOUR OF THE FUTURE by Mark Stevenson
Profile Books 2011.

Always lively and interesting, albeit undeniably alarming at times, this personal quest into what may lie ahead opens with a chapter on Transhumanism, and also looks at the possibilities and implications of nanotechnology.

THE TRANSHUMANIST READER by Max More and Natasha
Vita-More (eds)
Wiley-Blackwell 2013.
A primary reference point for Chapter Nine of *Inferno Decoded*,
containing 42 punchy essays and extracts that deal with the philosophy,
science, politics and technology of Transhumanism.

THE SINGULARITY IS NEAR by Ray Kurzweil
Duckworth Overlook 2005.
If anyone would know whether we're approaching the Singularity –
the moment when artificial intelligence definitively outstrips human
intelligence – it has to be Ray Kurzweil, who came up with the idea, and
was appointed Google's director of engineering in 2012. Dan Brown
specifically recommends Kurzweil's doorstop of a book to readers of
Inferno.

HUMANITY+
humanityplus.org
Humanity+ is a membership organisation of Transhumanists that
publishes H+ magazine, organises conferences and has local 'chapters'.
The FAQ section on its website covers all aspects of Transhumanist
philosophy.

FLORENCE

BLUE GUIDE FLORENCE by Alta Macadam
Blue Guides.
Alta Macadam has lived in the hills above Florence for many years and
knows the city inside out. Small wonder that Dan Brown cites the *Blue
Guide* as one of his sources for *Inferno*. Our map on p.203 is based, with
permission, on a map from this guidebook.

THE MUSEUMS OF FLORENCE
www.museumsinflorence.com
Not all of the seventy-two places covered on this site are what you
would think of as 'museums'. Most of the places mentioned in Dan
Brown's *Inferno* are here, including the Boboli Gardens, the Palazzo Pitti,
the Vasari Corridor, the Palazzo Vecchio and the Baptistery.

CONSTANTINOPLE

BYZANTIUM 1200
www.byzantium1200.com
This website provides three-dimensional recreations of Constantinople, today's Istanbul, including the Hagia Sophia.

THE WORKS OF DAN BROWN

DIGITAL FORTRESS, 1998	THE DA VINCI CODE, 2003
ANGELS AND DEMONS, 2000	THE LOST SYMBOL, 2009
DECEPTION POINT, 2001	INFERNO, 2013

www.danbrown.com
www.facebook.com/DanBrown
Dan Brown's own website has details of all the novels and film versions and a 'Secrets' feature where, if you type in the word 'Pythagoras' you go through to a video of Dan emerging through a 'secret door' in the Palazzo Vecchio in Florence. Or you could join the 2.6m visitors to Dan's Facebook site, where the author posts regular photos and text relating to his novels.

Index

Figures in *italics* refer to illustrations.

Printed in the United States
By Bookmasters